Go from romantic to

52 Saturday Nights

*Are your Saturday nights everything you want them to be?
With sexual sage Joan Elizabeth Lloyd as your guide,
you're about to plunge into fifty-two Saturday nights—one
entire year—of exciting new pleasures guaranteed to give
a new spin (and new sizzle) to "date night."*

❤♡ *Ask her to wear her sexiest underwear—or no
underwear at all—beneath her clothing so that all
day she'll think of you.*

❤♡ *Ask him to wear a ribbed or studded condom—
inside out.*

❤♡ *Skinny-dip at midnight in the backyard kiddie
wading pool.*

❤♡ *Fool around at the top of a Ferris wheel.*

❤♡ *Light a "magic" candle and say, "As long as it's lit,
you're mine to do with whatever I like."*

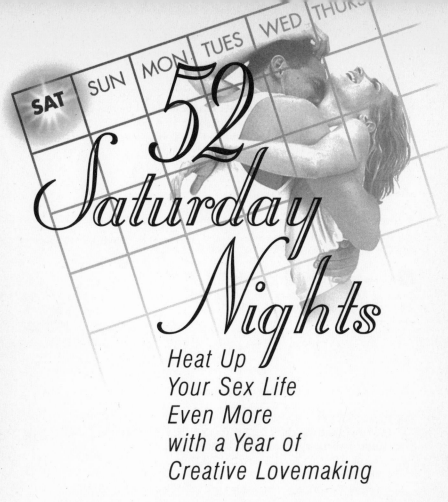

52 Saturday Nights

Heat Up
Your Sex Life
Even More
with a Year of
Creative Lovemaking

JOAN ELIZABETH LLOYD

WARNER BOOKS

A Time Warner Company

Warner Books, Inc., 1271 Avenue of the Americas, New York, NY 10020

Visit our Web site at www.twbookmark.com

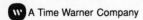 A Time Warner Company

Printed in the United States of America

First Printing: February 2000

10 9 8 7 6 5

Library of Congress Cataloging-in-Publication Data

Lloyd, Joan Elizabeth.
    Fifty-two Saturday nights : heat up your sex life even more with a year of creative lovemaking / Joan Elizabeth Lloyd.
        p. cm.
    ISBN 0-446-67629-2
    1. Sex instruction. 2. Sex in marriage. 3. Sexual excitement. I. Title.

HQ31 .L64 2000
613.9'6—dc21   99-044620

Book design and text composition by H. Roberts Design

Contents

Contents

Contents

52
Saturday
Nights

Introduction

h—Saturday night. A night for dates, laughs, fun, adventure. A night for letting go and for holding on. A night for fun with a long-standing partner or a date with someone new and exciting. A night for wonderful traditional lovemaking or for moving on to exciting new bedroom pastimes. A night for lovers.

But is your Saturday night everything you want it to be? Are your evenings pretty ordinary? Dinner at an Italian restaurant? A movie? Sitting on the couch watching reruns of *The Simpsons*? Do you spend your time shuttling the kids around? An evening with your folks? Bridge with the Martins? The late news? A quickie? A longie that's exactly like most of the other longies you and your partner share?

Not anymore. What follows are fifty-two Saturday nights filled with new ideas, old ideas with new twists, and opportunities to create excitement and romance. Fifty-two Saturday nights. One year. A year to relish new pleasures. A year of creative fun and new adventures. A year to build on the wonderful things you and your partner have or to find new pleasures with someone you might not have even met yet. A year of new discoveries. A year of carefully moving to something just a bit unusual or a year of plunging headlong into new activities. A year of practical advice, useful suggestions, creative ideas. A year of teases, tips, and temptations. A year of serious learning. A year of frolic. Each week, you'll find something new to read, to try, to learn. Each week, there will be something to make you smile, to make you thrill, to make you desire and to make you desirable. Together, we'll begin with the basics and then progress through the erotic to the exotic and unusual.

But all the new ideas in the world aren't going to help much if you don't actually do something with the new information. Years ago, during my first marriage, I read what books and magazine articles there were about how to spice up my love life. Most of the hints, tips, and tricks were, however, really intimidating. I wasn't going to discuss making love in the living room with my husband, certainly not when we had children who wandered the house at night. I wasn't about to visit him at work dressed in only a trench coat or suggest unusual sexual games. I didn't know how to mention it, and I had no idea how he would react. I'm sorry now that I didn't, because, although I'm not sure it would have lengthened our relationship, it certainly would have made our time together much more fun for both of us.

Maybe you're not so different, even in this age of enlightenment. I hear you. You're saying, "I don't think I can really invite my husband into my bubble bath. He'd never go for making love on the kitchen counter or in the car. It sounds like fun, but real people don't do that. Brushing my hair as foreplay? Not John. He's not like that. He's a 'Let's get to it' kind of guy." Well, I say to you, "Not nec-

essarily." You'll never know unless you give it a try, and I'll be here all year to help you. I'll suggest what to say, exactly what to do, and how to go about making it happen.

Read one selection for a Saturday night each week, or read the book all at once. Read by yourself or, better yet, read together. If you find something particularly delicious and have no idea how to carry the idea through, give it to your partner to read and then let nature take its course. If some of the ideas are exciting to read about but you wouldn't actually want to do them, share the section with your partner, while making it clear that this is for fantasy enjoyment only.

As you share some of the ideas with your partner, raise your radar antenna to the fullest. Try to catch the subtle clues about what turns him or her on. Try to send easy-to-catch messages about what you like. If you can't do it with words, use moans, sighs, and body movements. Help your partner as you wish your partner would help you. Good lovemaking involves both partners communicating and helping each other to create the best loving possible. Of course, I'll help you find new ways to do that, too.

So here, for you and your partner, are fifty-two Saturday nights of exciting new pleasures. Let's begin.

$\mathcal{S}aturday$ $\mathcal{N}ight \;\#\; 1$

Begin at the Beginning —of the Day

aking love. It probably begins with a touch, a glance, whatever signal you and your partner exchange as the evening progresses that says, Let's. But anticipation is one of the most delicious parts of any sexual encounter.

I'm sure you've read a novel or watched a movie or TV show in which there's a he and a she who you know will eventually end up in bed together. You avidly turn the pages or urge time to pass as you wait for the spark to become a flame. Everything that they do leading up to the "big moment" increases the sexual tension, for them and for you. Anticipation! It can be like that for you and your partner.

But shouldn't sex be spontaneous? Sure—why not? Spontaneity is wonderful. Coming home from work, dragging your partner into the bedroom, and ripping all of your clothes off can be wonderful. Deciding in the middle of a movie that you need to be home, *now,* is deliciously erotic. But planning a night of making love and letting your partner in on the plan can be just as arousing.

How? Let's begin this, our first Saturday night together, with the idea that tonight's the night. Begin at the very start of the day. When you wake up Saturday morning, whisper in your partner's ear that you have something sexually exciting planned for that evening. "Not now," you say, jumping out of bed, "but later. Think about it." Do you have to have something really different planned? Not necessarily. The difference will be the anticipation and the arousal that your comment stimulates.

For Her

❤♡ Put a ribbon or rubber band around his wrist, just below his wristwatch, so that every time he checks the time, he's reminded that something good is in store. Make a cassette with some erotic music, something that's meaningful to you both, and slip it into his car stereo for him to listen to as he does his errands. It can be anything from Michael Bolton to Beethoven, so long as it sends a message. If you're really creative, include a few well-chosen words with the music that hint at the evening's activities. A single word or an entire erotic scenario? That's up to you.

If you lay out his clothes in the morning, select something he knows you find arousing, like a particularly tight T-shirt or a pair of black briefs. As he's dressing, slip a piece of satin or canvas or a small piece of fur into the crotch of his shorts so that he feels it all day and thinks of you.

Do you make his lunch? Put something suggestive in for a snack, with a note saying, "I hear that olives make you passionate. Let's hope that's true, because I have designs on your body tonight."

For Him

❤♡ Call her up during the day and whisper a few naughty words about the evening to come. That can be particularly delicious if she's in a roomful of people and can't react. Create a pet name that you only use in the dark. Ed calls me a "sexy bitch," abbreviated SB, and when I hear that, I know he's having wonderfully erotic thoughts. If you also explain to the kids that SB stands for "silly beast," only the two of you will know its sexual connotation. Call her that all day.

Pull a particularly sexy piece of underwear from her drawer and ask her to wear it for you beneath her clothing so that all day she'll think of you. Ask her to shorten her bra straps so they bind a bit at the shoulder.

For Both of You

❤♡ If you can, plan to have dinner out that evening. Draw out the suspense with a long meal, with lots of suggestive gazes, comments, and gestures. Remember, we're trying to make the excitement last as long as possible.

For Fun

❤♡ If you're really daring, take a slender ribbon and run it through one of the leg holes of a pair of briefs or panties (it works

7

equally well with either), then through the waist opening. Tie the ribbon tightly; then do the same at the other side of the undies. Now the crotch of the pants will be really binding and uncomfortable in an erotic way. Then ask your partner to wear them so he or she will think about you all day. That constant reminder will make your lover so hungry that by the time the day comes to an end, it will be all you can do to postpone the inevitable until bedtime.

But who wants to postpone it anyway? Remember spontaneity?

Saturday Night #2

The Perfect Kiss

Kissing. A wonderful pleasure. It's unfortunate that after awhile, kissing gets to be perfunctory. In moving on toward a goal, we forget that the stops along the way frequently hold the most allure. Has kissing become something you and your partner do to "get there"? Or is your kissing limited to a "Hi, honey" peck on the cheek?

Let's use this Saturday night to practice the delicious art of kissing. Is there a perfect kiss? Certainly, but it's different for every couple, a personal thing between you and your partner. Although there are good kissers and poor kissers, the best kiss is one that's been practiced between lovers, lingered over, and savored.

For tonight, kissing will be our focus. Long, delicious, soul-searing kisses that weaken the knees and quicken the pulse. Kisses that are more than a meeting of mouths, ones that are slow journeys from erotic spot to erotic spot, with soft, warm lips creating new and delightful pathways.

Begin with the face, kissing each other's closed eyes, ears, cheeks, slowly tasting each sensual spot. Linger over the hairline, eyebrows, tip of the nose. If something tickles, smile, giggle, and then move on. Each lover is the giver and receiver of kisses, and it is all slow, the aim being to tempt, to seduce.

Move on to the mouth, gently tasting each other. Deepen the kiss, lip to lip, tongue to tongue, exploring each other. Linger, letting tension build. Use your lips, keeping them moving, opening and closing, touching and tasting. Cup his or her face with your hands, changing position to deepen the sensations.

Tiny bites can be arousing, and that's the idea. Nibble at your partner's lips, tiny nips, to change the sensation, and then kiss where you've just nibbled. Lick your partner's lips, too, using the flat of your tongue or just the tiniest tip. Tease. Kiss deeply, and then just brush your lips ever so softly over your partner's.

Relax. Use your tongue as a temptation. I've kissed men who stick their tongues out as if they're about to say *Ahhh* at the doctor's, then stuff them down my throat. Tongues are soft and gentle. You can suck on your partner's gently or even bite it a bit. Use your tongue to taste; feel the different textures of your partner's mouth. Explore his or her teeth, cheeks, lips, and tongue. A simple rule of thumb is to kiss the way you'd like to be kissed.

While you're kissing, try opening your eyes. It's a delight to see how much your lover is enjoying the experience, the depth of emotion, and the heat. You can even ask your partner to open his or her eyes so that you can gaze at each other while indulging.

Let your lips wander. I particularly like to be kissed and nibbled on the tender spot where the side of my neck joins my shoulder. Others find the nape of the neck or the hollow at the base of the throat thrilling. Be at your most aware and you'll quickly discover what makes your partner sizzle. Then do more. Keep turning up the heat!

Don't forget to use the warmth of your breath to arouse. The old "Blow in my ear and . . ." may be a cliché, but there's a reason for it. Licking, kissing, and nipping at your partner's ear is thrilling, and the heat of your fevered breathing will add fuel to the growing fire.

Remember not to let your hands remain idle while kissing, but don't get grabby and rush on to those "erogenous zones." Rather, stroke your lover's back or shoulders, cup his or her chin or the back of the neck, tangle your fingers in your partner's hair, and even pull slightly without hurting.

Let your bodies press against each other as you kiss. Relax into the embrace and move closer, and closer still, until the entire length of you is pressed against the entire length of your lover. Sigh, purr, growl.

For Her

♥Move so your breasts brush against his chest, through his clothing. Tip your pelvis so your pubic mound presses against his erection. Let him know that you know that he's excited and that the fact pleases you. If you've got nails, use them. Softly scratch the back of his neck. Be a bit aggressive if you like. Let him know you want him.

Really good kissing is an all-but-lost art. Kisses have become matter-of-fact and common. Change that tonight. If you need inspiration, think about some great screen kisses like the ones in *Titanic, Ghost, Top Gun, Body Heat,* and *Basic Instinct.* Those are really hot, and you can be, too.

For Him

❤️Holding her gently, let her feel the hardness of your arousal. Use a hand in the small of her back to press your groin lightly against hers. Don't grind. The area over the pubic bone can be quite sensitive, and if you're too aggressive, it will hurt. But it's a great thrill for a woman to know that she's excited her lover. Don't hesitate to let her know you want her and want to go further. But, again, don't rush or insist. Remember that the key words for tonight are *savor* and *linger.*

For Both of You

❤️Stolen kisses in almost-public places can be delightful. A quick peck at a stoplight on the way to a party can give an evening an erotic start. A sudden lick on the back of the neck while your partner's getting something out of the refrigerator or washing the dishes is quite a change of pace. Don't miss out on an opportunity for a brief smack or a long, erotic kiss. It's all wonderful, whether it's followed up by lovemaking or not.

For Fun

❤️Ladies, do you have any flavored lip gloss? A quick application can make kissing all the more delicious.

Saturday Night #3

Doing Everything But . . .

ow to Climax Every Time." "The Twenty-Minute Orgasm."
"How to Reach the Heights of Ecstasy at 30,000 Feet." Magazine
articles, books, and talk shows all discuss, at great length, how to
achieve orgasm, as if orgasm were the ultimate goal, the only
thing about a sexual evening worth mentioning.

Hogwash. I get so upset as I look at the magazine racks, imagining the zillions of men and women who think that orgasm is *it*.
Don't get me wrong: Orgasm is wonderful. It's a terrific culmination of a wonderful sexual evening. But it's not the be-all and end-
all. It's the lovemaking that makes an evening memorable, not the
end result.

Remember when you were first dating, before you made love
for the first time? Remember how aroused you got as the evening
progressed, even though you knew that the two of you wouldn't

end up in bed together? And remember how wonderful you felt later? Obviously, that enjoyment had nothing to do with orgasm. So tonight, let's not worry about the destination, but savor the trip, the lovemaking.

Spend time this evening making love, without any concern about climax. Touch, dance, caress, nibble, talk dirty, tell stories, gaze at a catalog of sex toys, but relish the journey and ignore the destination. Make a vow that you're going to spend until, say, 11:00 P.M. just making love, without any rush toward orgasm. Set a timer if you want and promise no touching genitals until it goes off. I'll bet that by the time you hear the ding, you'll both be so hot and bothered that you'll probably rip each other's clothes off. But remember, that's not the object of the game. The journey is.

Cuddling. It's a singular pleasure, often overlooked in the rush to consummation. Holding, stroking, feeling the length of your body against the length of your partner's can create a closeness that's loving and tender. Ed and I like spooning. Ed turns on his side and curls slightly; then I press my body against his back, matching the curl of his legs, my arm around his waist, touching whatever I want to touch. After awhile, we reverse so that he's against my back, touching me. We're as close as two spoons in a drawer. Somehow when we talk, cuddled like that, everything's so much more intimate.

Your partner isn't into cuddling, you say. He or she just rolls over and goes to sleep. Well, if you want snuggling, ask for it. Don't assume any hostility on your lover's part. He or she probably just hasn't thought much about that part of sex. So say, "Hey, baby, roll over here and let's hug for a few minutes." Saying "I'd love to feel your arms around me" or "I really enjoy falling asleep all tangled together" will also let your partner know you'd enjoy this.

For Fun

❤♡ Share the lounge chair while you watch TV. Get as much of your body in contact with your partner's body as possible. Or let one sit on the other's lap in a rocker. The motion of the chair is both soothing and erotic.

When you're ready for bed, undress each other slowly, but no overt sexual touching. Enjoy the experience, each button, each hook or zipper. Treasure every inch of skin as it's revealed.

For Fun

❤♡ Decide that you're going to make love this evening but not climax—neither of you. Concentrate on the fun of the experience, the textures, the tastes. You may even decide to go to sleep without climaxing. Of course, what happens when you wake up at three o'clock in the morning is up to you.

There are many who enjoy a special and slightly unusual pleasure. When a couple is ready for sleep, the man inserts his penis into the woman, but then they just lie there, tangled together, and eventually drift off, feeling the complete closeness, but without orgasm. It takes some mental discipline, but it might be worth a try tonight.

Saturday Night # 4

The Greatest Natural Aphrodisiac

I have asked lots of people to try to tell me what makes someone sexually irresistible. After lots of conversations and E-mail, I've finally been able to qualify what people think. The greatest natural aphrodisiac seems to be your partner's desire for you. At first, I thought that wasn't what I was looking for. I expected people to talk about buns, hands, eyes, or breasts, but most of the people I asked wound up talking about desire. "The knowledge that someone wants me, specifically me and not merely someone to make love to, acts on my body like a chemical," one woman said. "It's like I've taken some kind of aphrodisiac." As I thought about it, I had to agree.

I soon realized that that's the quality that sexy movie stars and singers have. Although they are singing or performing for vast, often unseen, audiences, they make me feel that they are focused on me. It's that ability to make me feel I'm wanted and needed—that he would climb mountains, give up kingdoms, whatever, just for me—that turns me to mush.

You don't have kingdoms to give up for your partner, of course, nor do you have to swim great rivers just to be together. But you do have the ability to make your lover the center of your evening.

For Both of You

❤Forget the rest of the world for this Saturday night. Chuck thoughts of the kids, the job, the house, the relatives. If those thoughts sneak into your mind, squash them. Think only of your partner's desires and needs. Concentrate. I know it's difficult, because you are probably out of the habit. Consider this. When you go out for dinner, what do you usually talk about? How about in the car? I thought so. Okay, don't do it.

What to talk about instead? How about talking about the things that are important to your partner? How did you enjoy the TV show last night? Did you like the dinner? What would you do with a million dollars if you had it? Where would you like to be in five years? If you want to talk about sex, you can start by discussing what both of you find sexy in a partner. What clothes, or lack of them, turn you on? Focus carefully on the answers. Listen, not with jealousy, but with creativity. You might learn lots of things that will help you plan a sexy future evening. Does he like tight T-shirts? Does she like the look of a man in a suit? Now you've got an idea what to wear next Saturday night.

For Her

❤If he's a sports fan and you can tolerate, say, basketball, get tickets to a game. Put them in an envelope and present them to him as

17

a special gift as you're leaving the house. You might enclose a pair of your panties in the envelope, too. Tell him that you'll probably be in such a hurry to dress that you might forget to wear any. That ought to make him think about you during halftime. But go along and enjoy what he enjoys. The lovemaking later will be a fringe benefit.

For Him

♥♡ If she wants to go to a fancy restaurant, make reservations. Don't grumble about having to wear a suit; do it for her. Focus on her. Maybe, as you're waiting for dessert, ask her to go into the ladies' room and take off her bra, just for you. Or remove your shorts in the men's room and hand them to her as a trophy. Desire. Wanting. Share it; it's a precious gift.

For Both of You

♥♡ Whatever you're doing, hold hands. Gaze into your partner's eyes, holding that gaze just a bit longer than you might otherwise. Stroke the palm of his or her hand with your finger, slowly and sensuously circling, so that only the two of you know.

Center your attention on your partner, keeping the conversation light but personal. Compliment your lover, but keep it genuine and not overblown. Don't say, "You look fabulous." Rather, mention something specific: "I love that color on you" or "That neckline shows off your lovely breasts." Try saying, "Your hands are so sexy that I find myself picturing them on my body" or "You've got such a sensuous mouth, so kissable." This last one will be even sexier if you then slowly suck a bite of gooey chocolate cake off your fork or take a small nibble of an after-dinner mint.

Touch in secret. As you're helping her with her coat, brush her breast. If you walk up behind him, kiss the back of his neck. If you're going to a movie, nibble at your partner's earlobe in the dark. Play, but don't hesitate to let your desire show.

Whisper sweet nothings. What are nothings? You might say, "I can't wait to get you home so I can . . . " You can fill in the rest. Or "Remember last Saturday night how I . . . " You get it. Is it embarrassing? Maybe a little. You're letting it all out, but the rewards can be amazing.

For Fun

Call your partner from the supermarket or hardware store on Saturday afternoon. Tell your lover that you're thinking about him or her and how much you're anticipating your evening together. Has your partner got a cell phone? A surprise phone call to say you want to be together can make all the difference.

For Fun

Is there a playground in your neighborhood that's available after dark? If there is, wander over and play. Swing together on the swings. One of you push the other, maybe from the front. Slide down the slide and let your partner catch you. Sit in the sandbox together, but tonight, and every night, make your hunger for your partner evident.

Desire. It's the best aphrodisiac there is.

19

Saturday Night #5

Nighttime Whispers

The key to making your sexual relationship better than it is now is communication. Unfortunately, for many couples, it seems to be a more difficult skill than any other. Almost every week, I receive a letter from someone, male or female, who's reluctant to try something new for fear of not doing it right. I answer each letter in a similar fashion: Ask your partner to help you. How? How can you help your partner to do it better? It's not as difficult as you might think. Imagine how wonderful it would feel if your partner behaved in the ways I suggest. You can ask for it, you know. Tonight, let's focus on how to tell your lover what you really want.

Don't worry about insulting your lover by telling him or her how it might be better. I know your lover will appreciate the help. Wouldn't you? Better sex is the object of the game, and whatever makes that happen is wonderful.

For Both of You

❤First, be sure to inform your partner of what feels best. Notice that I use the word *inform*, not *tell*, because a good way to start is by nonverbal means. Moan, purr, move in such a way that it's obvious what he or she is doing feels good. Help your partner. You might have actually been holding back. Women in particular believe that they must be silent in the bedroom. Nonsense. Sigh, moan, yell. Don't scream, of course, when you can be overheard (unless that's to both of your tastes), but let your partner know.

The next step is to use a few well-chosen words—yes, *words*—to tell him or her how good things feel. Try saying, "That feels wonderful" or "Oh, do more of that." Say, "Don't stop," "Good," or "Yes, baby." You will reap the rewards immediately.

Use your body to help your partner know where to touch. Take your partner's hand and move it where you want it. Cover that hand with your own and guide it. Haven't there been times when you've been hesitant to try something and really wanted help? I'm sure there have. Wouldn't you have liked some guidance? Now you help your lover the way you've always wanted to be helped. Then you can ask for it for yourself. "Please help me; show me what pleases you." Or "I want to give you pleasure, but I'm not sure how."

If you've made it this far, maybe you can take it one step further. You could say, "Have you ever done anything in bed that you didn't enjoy or that didn't work out the way you thought it would?" Negatives make a question easier to answer than asking, "What do you like?" Maybe start by volunteering something of your own. I remember going to bed with a man who smoked. It was in 1981, when I was doing a lot of short-term dating and having one-night stands. His smoking didn't bother me when we met, but once in bed, I couldn't abide it. I've tried making love standing up or with my back against a wall, and that never worked. I've had rug burns on my spine, and once I threw my back out during some particularly strenuous gymnastics.

Okay now, how brave are you feeling? In the dark, during lovemaking or after, ask your partner whether he or she has any fantasy that has never been acted upon. Phew, that's a tough question to answer honestly. I believe we all have secret desires, and we may prefer that many of them remain secret. But I've shared many of my fantasies with Ed and he has shared with me. We've played several of them out, and most of them have been just great. I do, however, have a few secrets, even after fourteen years of storytelling.

But practically, how do you discuss something so basic, even with a lifetime mate? Be brave and start small. "I've always wanted to make love outdoors." Or "I've wanted to do it with the lights on." Don't spoil things by discussing your fantasies of Sean Penn or Pamela Lee Anderson. This isn't the time or place. (There may be no time or place for discussing fantasies about other people.) But if you keep it simple, you probably have one you can mention.

One way to reveal a desire is to tell a story. A common fantasy is to be marooned, just you two, in some cabin in the woods. What would you do then? Use that idea to start a story. "Maybe we're snowed in with lots of food and firewood, but the roads are closed and won't be open for several days. What should we do? How about lying by the fireplace and I'll take off my shirt? . . ." You can slip in ideas without it feeling too personal.

Another? "I'm a stranger and I'm walking home. You've been watching me and wondering what it would be like to take off my clothes. Suddenly, a storm comes up and, as I walk by your

house, you see me, soaked to the skin, and invite me in where it's warm. . . ."

Another? "Maybe I'm sitting in a bar and you sit beside me and buy me a drink. I've had a few and you tell me that your apartment is right around the corner. . . ."

You can get as creative as you want. A good idea is to stop the story at some delicious point and ask your partner, "What do you think happens then?" That can allow almost anyone to talk about some deep, sexy thought with little risk of rejection.

In several later selections, I'll help you by giving you story starters like these to work from. They will be longer, with involved setups to get you started. Telling fantasies in the dark can help you explore areas you've never talked about before. What a joy!

For Fun

❤During lovemaking, get graphic in describing how excited you are. "You make me so hot." Or "God, your sexy body really turns me on. I can't wait much longer to love you." How about saying, "Do it, now!" or "Wrap your legs around my waist so I can be deeper inside of you!"

For Fun

❤While telling a story, slip in one of those four-letter words your parents used to threaten to wash your mouth out for using. You'll be surprised by the erotic stimulation a well-placed "Oh, baby, I love it when you fuck me" adds. You could say, "I love the feeling of your hard cock inside of me." Or "Your sweet tits are so kissable."

23

Saturday Night #6

Clothes Make the Man—or Woman

*T*onight's a night for loving, and you want to send the message that you're in the mood. What can you wear that sends the right signals, either to your husband of twenty or thirty years or to a date, a new and sexy partner with whom you want to go further?

For Her

We think that men want their women naked, but wearing something provocative can press the right buttons even more. Remember how tempting movie queens were in the forties and fifties, before anyone was allowed to actually expose anything? That's the idea. A little something is so much sexier than nothing, and it's an invitation to your partner to expose what's underneath. Later.

For starters, keep it simple. Wear something just a bit tighter than usual. Unbutton an extra button of your blouse. Treat yourself to a Wonderbra that can make your cleavage shadowy and mysterious.

If you don't have a lot of money, borrow something from a friend, or wander through garage sales to find something a bit unlike the usual you. Go to the local discount store and, as you prowl the aisles, let your mind wander. Pick up an inexpensive chain, long enough that a heavy bauble will fall right in your cleavage, or a sheer blouse that leaves just a bit to the imagination. I remember one daring blouse I had. It was almost transparent, but it had pockets of extrathick fabric that just covered my breasts. It made my date crazy!

Shoes? Wear slip-on shoes so you can get barefoot. Why not paint your toenails a daring shade of red? If you have or can find them, a pair of strappy sandals with outrageous heels might be just the thing. I had a pair of red ones I used to call my "whorehouse shoes." I was sure if I ever walked any distance in them, I'd break an ankle, so I only wore them around the house. But that was enough.

Another dress I remember zipped up the front. I would wear it to a party; then I had lots of fun slowly unzipping, a half an inch at a time as the evening progressed. It never got indecent, just provocative, and I made sure my date noticed.

When you're feeling a bit bolder, how about removing your bra or panties sometime during the evening? And be sure your partner knows what you've done. If you can, do it at a party or someplace where he can't act on the natural urge right then. Let him think about it for a while. Then, when you get home, you won't be able to get to the bedroom fast enough.

For the truly adventurous, if you're looking for an evening where he takes control, get a small padlock, like the ones that come on suitcases, and put it on a bracelet in the morning. Then give him the key, to be used that evening for whatever he wants to lock up.

For Her

❤♡ There are stores in almost every mall in which you can have clasps put on chains of any length. How about getting one an inch or two longer than your waist and wearing it beneath your jeans? Won't he be surprised!

Remember that whatever you wear, you're sending a message that you're trying to look sexy for your partner. I will guarantee that the effort will be greatly appreciated.

For Him

❤♡ Men look really sexy in anything with a jacket—that's why women like men in military uniforms. I know you probably hate to wear a jacket in the evening. Either you wear one all day or you never wear one, but it's really attractive. And while you're dancing, she can slip her hand beneath it, to where it's warm and inviting.

Tight T-shirts are really sexy, at least to me, especially those body-hugging, muscle-man ones. Rummage through the back of your closet for something from your dating years. I'll bet you looked and felt sexy then. Find something that makes you feel like a Lothario, a lady-killer, and then wear it. Flaunt it!

Do you remember Harry Belafonte at his sexiest? I had delicious fantasies about him after seeing his gorgeous chest exposed by those unbuttoned shirts. Leather is also really erotic and may be a completely different style for you. If you've got an old leather vest, wear that, with no shirt. Sure you can.

Use a bit of cologne after dinner, especially if you're staying home. The nose is a sex organ, you know, and taking that extra bit of care shows her that it matters to you how she perceives you.

For Both of You

❤♡ Realize that it's the effort you're making and the message you're sending that's so much more important than how you look. Don't think about extra pounds or the signs of age. Think about trying to tell your partner, by what you're wearing, that you're anxious to spend an evening making long, slow love. What could be better?

For Fun

❤♡ Ever played dress up? Do it tonight. If you two have a favorite fantasy, dress accordingly. Doctor's scrubs or a peasant blouse and gaudy earrings, a toy gun and holster or a plain white cotton bra and panties—all these set the scene for playing out a fantasy. Tight leather pants? A corset? Swashbuckling tight jeans, boots, and a flowing shirt? A garter belt and seamed stockings?

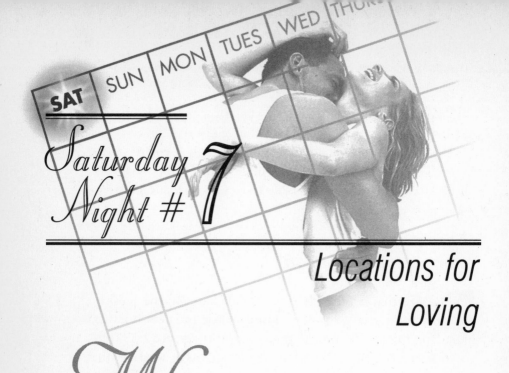

Saturday Night # 7

Locations for Loving

W here do you make love? I can hear you now. "We do it in the bedroom, of course." Well, not of course. Tonight, let's explore the myriad locations for loving. Start somewhere tonight; then make a vow to make love in every other room of the house before next Saturday.

In the Kitchen

Have you ever considered that the counters in the average kitchen are at a great height for sex? If your partner sits on the cool surface with his or her legs spread, you can touch, lick, or penetrate whatever you please. And, of course, if you want to cover your lover's body with appetizing goodies first, you have easy access to all the delicious possibilities in the cabinets and the refrigerator. Strawberry jam, anyone? What can you do with a well-washed cucumber or carrot?

For Her

❤♡ Got an orange? Cut a wide hole in one end and impale his erection with it. It's an amazing sensation and licking the juice off is another treat.

For Him

❤♡ Have your partner sit with her feet in the sink and aim the vegetable sprayer between her legs. Take care not to soak the floor, or just don't worry about it and mop up later.

In the Living Room

With a little imagination, coffee tables can become sex toys. If she lies across the table, facedown, her knees on the floor, her hands holding two of the legs, she's delightfully displayed for loving. I have a glass coffee table. It would feel tantalizingly cold, and I wonder what Ed would see from beneath. If your partner lies on the table, faceup, you can straddle the table and him at the same time. And what will you two be thinking the next time your mother-in-law puts her coffee cup down on the surface?

For Fun

❤♡ Here's an idea for those of you with camping equipment. Pitch your tent on the living room floor. It creates an intimate cocoon for the two of you. Got a sleeping bag? Zip the two of you into it and let nature take its course.

In the Garage

Got a pickup truck? Ever done it in the truck bed? You can give the springs quite a workout. Or have you ever done it on the workbench? What's in the toolbox that you can play with?

Outside

There's always a lawn chair, but here's an even better erotic idea. Got a swing set in the backyard and some privacy? Have your partner sit on the swing, without undies, with his or her feet on the seat, knees raised. Then push the swing from the front. Every time your lover swings toward you, lick or suck something. Hold the swing high in the air and enjoy. Eventually, you might like to sit together on the swing and rock while you make love.

For Fun

♥♡ Have you got a small wading pool for the kids? Splashing around nude in the dark can lead to all kinds of new pleasures.

In the Dining Room

Those wonderful wooden armchairs make wonderful places for sex.

For Fun

♥ He sits on one, his erection poking up from his groin. She sits on his lap, facing him, and impales herself. Now have a contest. Each of you can play with the other. Hands and mouths are allowed, but no hip movement is permitted. Whoever moves or climaxes first, when the teasing gets to be too much, loses. What's the prize? Does it matter?

For Fun

♥ Put your lover in the chair beneath the brightest light you have. The heat will add to the sensations.

In the Den

Have you got a rocking chair or a lounger? Those are great places for sport. And hassocks are soft and low enough to create a new atmosphere. So are piano benches.

For Fun

♥ Here's a silly idea. One person takes a heavy book in each hand and doesn't let go. Let the other person do whatever sexy things he or she can think of to make you drop the book. Who wins and who loses? Who cares?

In the Bathroom

Making love in the tub or shower is a common occurrence. Here are a few more exotic ideas.

For Her

♥♡How about letting your partner judge his own personal wet T-shirt contest? Wear an old one, but nothing else; then get wet in the shower. Let him use his hands or mouth to measure your assets.

For Fun

♥♡Shower in the dark and fumble for the soap. You know it's there somewhere. Just feel around. Use the loofah, too.

For Fun

♥♡Position your partner on the bathroom counter and make love while you both watch in the bathroom mirror. (More about mirrors on Saturday Night #44.)

In the Rec Room

Have you got a bar? Have you ever made love on it, or on one of those bar stools?

For Fun

❤️Got a liqueur collection? Try out different concoctions to enhance the taste of sex. Fill your mouth with crème de menthe, Kahlúa, Amaretto, or Cointreau; then lick some part of your partner's body. You might have to shower later, but that's another sport.

For Fun

❤️What kind of play equipment do you have for the kids? A trampoline? A small plastic slide? Open the toy box and get creative.

In the Bedroom

Let's decide not to make love on the bed this time. Instead, spread lots of pillows on the floor and fool around there. A note: When you make love on a floor, take care to avoid rug burns. Make sure there's a pillow or towel beneath the buttocks of whoever's on the bottom. I've gotten several nasty abrasions on my coccyx, although I was unaware of any problem until afterward.

So now you see that the bedroom isn't the only place for great sex. Your entire house is a playground. Use it—tonight and for the rest of the week.

Saturday Night #8

Condoms as Sex Toys

Condoms. Since condoms are your first line of defense against pregnancy and the spread of disease, the use of condoms usually falls under the heading "If I really must!" But it doesn't have to be that way. Using a condom can be part of your evening's sexual enjoyment. Tonight, let's explore how to use condoms as a fun part of lovemaking.

Why use a condom? If you and your partner haven't been together and exclusively so for at least five years, or if you haven't had a definitive AIDS test, condoms are a must. Even if you are HIV-negative, if you want to prevent the spread of other sexually transmitted diseases like chlamydia and gonorrhea, then, again, condoms are necessary. In addition, condoms are effective in preventing unwanted pregnancy.

Okay, I hear you. You're convinced that you and your partner should be using condoms, but it's still something you'd rather avoid. It's your body, of course, so you can and will do as you choose. But it's possible to make condoms part of your sexual routine.

First, select the right kind of condom. A few actually come in different sizes, so be sure that the type you and your partner select is the proper girth. It's nice to think that he's got the biggest equipment ever and he needs the "supermanly" size, but if it slips off midintercourse, it's useless. Likewise, if you get one that's too small, it will slow the circulation (which may actually be a good thing—see below).

Condoms come in various textures, with ribs on the sides or ticklers on the end. Ed and I have tried different types (don't you just love research?) and I haven't been able to feel any difference. Ed says that the most important thing is to get condoms that are thin enough so they don't completely mute the sensations.

For Fun

❤ I haven't found that ribbed or studded condoms feel any different to me, but they do feel very different for a man, if worn inside out. With the textured surface against the penis, every thrust gives a massage.

Natural skin condoms are thinner than latex ones, but they do not prevent the passage of the AIDS virus. If you're not worried about disease and are just using condoms as a method of birth control, then those are just fine. Take care with latex condoms. Baby oil, Vaseline, and other products containing petroleum will break down the latex and create microscopic holes through which viruses can pass. If a lubricant is desired, you can get prelubricated condoms, or use special water-based products formulated for use with condoms. K-Y jelly, Astroglide, Probe, or Aqua Lube work well, and they differ slightly in feel and smell, so try out several and then choose the one you like best.

Don't use that condom that you've had in the drawer since you were dating. If a condom is more than a few months old, it might be over the hill and not do its job. Get fresh ones and throw the old ones out.

In order to be effective, a condom must be used properly. I know it seems like a simple thing, but many people don't follow all the instructions. Nothing more than unrolling it over the erect penis and you're ready. Right? Almost. First, be sure to use the condom before any (and I mean *any*) genital-to-genital contact. Massaging a woman's external tissues with a man's unprotected erection spreads as many viruses and as many sperm as you might get with actual penetration. Next, the condom must be unrolled completely over the penis, not just partway down. If the condom is too short or not unrolled completely, whatever is trapped in the latex will spill out into the vaginal canal. When unrolled, there must be a pocket at the tip to hold the fluids. If not, the fluids will be forced down the shaft and will ooze out.

A condom must remain covering the penis until the covered member is removed from the vagina, preferably while the penis is still partly erect. If the penis becomes completely flaccid, fluid can seep out of the condom and spread onto vaginal tissues. When he withdraws, it's important for one of you to hold the base of the condom against the penis and pull both out together. A condom that's left inside and then removed separately will inevitably leak.

Okay, okay. I hear you. I still haven't told you how to make condoms part of tonight's sex play.

For Her

❤️ Ask him to let you help; then unroll that little devil over his cock, ever so slowly, stroking and squeezing as you do it. Grasp the shaft and rub your hand up and down while "fumbling" with the latex. It's a game, but that's the idea. Say, "I'm afraid it's not going to go on too easily without some lubrication"; then lick the tip of his erection to "make it easier." Use a flavored lubricant and, as you're slowly spreading it over his shaft, lick some of it off. You don't have to deep-throat him, just lick his penis like it's an all-day sucker.

For Her

❤️ Go an erotic step further and, after the condom's partly on, unroll the rest with your tongue. It's silly, awkward, and fun. If you're worried that it won't taste nice, put a Life Saver in your mouth first. This is also a great way to try out oral sex without some of the associated reluctance.

For Him

❤️ Have you ever had a problem with climaxing too soon? I get dozens of letters from men who worry that they reach orgasm too quickly. Well, here's a way to solve that problem. Use a condom or, if you already use one, add a second, or try one that seems smaller around and thus tighter. This does two things. It slows the circulation to the penis and can help you maintain your erection longer, and it numbs the sensations so they aren't quite as intense. This has the wonderful benefit that it allows you to keep intercourse going longer. How great is that?

For Both of You

❤♡If you've never tried a prelubricated condom, you're both in for a treat. The cold feel of the gel adds an extra sensation that's really erotic.

For Both of You

❤♡Get several different kinds of condoms, gift wrap them, and have a "condom comparison." There are dozens to choose from. Your local variety store will have a few kinds, but those are pretty standard. I checked my local convenience store and it had both nonlubricated and lubricated ones, condoms that were mint-flavored and ones with ribs.

There are lots more options. You can get them in colors, including red, blue, yellow, and black; some are scented, including orange, banana, and strawberry fragrances. They also come in flavors. How about using your mouth to put on a chocolate-, mint-, or vanilla-flavored condom? Makes it seem more appealing, doesn't it?

Condoms that glow in the dark or that come with pictures that appear when the condom is unrolled onto a fully erect penis are also available. I saw ones advertised with the likenesses of Steve Austin of WWF fame, Marilyn Monroe, and the Chippendale dancers. Whatever you enjoy is great, and sometimes ridiculous is terrific.

If you want to get experimental, every adult toy store stocks several kinds. Major catalogs advertise several different brands and most offer assortments so you can experiment. We'll talk about catalogs later in the book, but for now, if you want to get one, try Condomania at 647 North Poinsettia Place, Los Angeles, CA 90036, or check in the appendix at the back of this book for addresses.

In addition to catalogs, there are several places on the Internet where you can get condoms of all kinds. We'll also talk later on about using the Internet, but for those of you who have access, let me mention two Web sites: Condom Sense at http://www.condoms.com and Condomania at http://www.condomania.com.

View this as scientific fun. Use a condom and then discuss the good and bad points. Talk in detail about how it felt, for both of you before, during, and after. Then make a few notes, maybe on the wrapper. When the lovemaking mood strikes again, use a different kind and again "analyze" the results. Remember, the more often you test your theories, the better the experiment (wink). Just remember to talk about it as if it's enjoyable, not some kind of punishment. It's all in the attitude.

Saturday Night #9

Quick Summer Sizzlers

Here are a few ideas to spice up a summer (or any other) Saturday.

- ♡ Sleep outdoors in a tent or just on several blankets in the backyard. If possible, select a night with a full moon and make love by moonlight.
- ♡ Eat a Popsicle together and lick the cold liquid from each other's fingers. And don't forget chins and lips.
- ♡ Skinny-dip in a lake, a friend's pool, or even the kids' wading pool on a hot Saturday night.
- ♡ Cover the sheets with talcum powder and roll around in it.
- ♡ For her: Get a pair of baby-doll pajamas and wear them. For him: Wearing just pajamas bottoms might drive her crazy.
- ♡ Get out the blender, lots of ice cubes, rum, and whatever

else tickles your fancy. Icy summer drinks are great heater-uppers.

♡ Try some crème de menthe on the rocks. I like the white kind, but the green is good, too.

♡ If you can't get outdoors, open the windows in the bedroom. Let the glow of the moonlight illuminate your naked skin. But don't shout too loudly when you climax. Your neighbors might not understand.

♡ Go to a fair or amusement park and neck at the top of the Ferris wheel.

♡ Write something really naughty in the sand. Then do it.

♡ Eat a really ripe mango or peach and let the juices drip everywhere. Forget the napkin; let your lover use his or her tongue.

♡ Wear your partner's shirt so that you're surrounded by your lover's personal scent.

♡ Do something you've never done together. Walk barefoot in the moonlight in the backyard. Take a cool shower together.

♡ Buy lots of flowers and fill the bedroom. Find a few wilted ones (they have the most scent), crush the petals in your hands, and sprinkle the soft scented bits on the bed.

♡ Sit quietly beside the ocean or a lake and just listen to the sounds of the water, the birds. Smell the air. Heighten your senses. Do you get a whiff of his aftershave or her perfume?

♡ I know it sounds corny, but take a long walk in the country. Hold hands. Stop frequently to sit and talk about sexy things. It really does perk up the libido. Then find the highest spot around and watch the sun set.

♡ Have a late-night picnic in the yard. Pack a basket with champagne and finger food and, while you eat, watch the stars and listen to the night sounds.

♡ Create a living sundae. Cover your lover's belly with whipped cream and a cherry. Then indulge.

♡ Take a walk in the dark; then find a spot and touch your lover all over. Worried that someone might see? That might make things even hotter.

♡ Put a bottle of body lotion in the refrigerator and then give your partner a massage.

♡ Feed each other strawberries dipped in chocolate sauce or frozen yogurt, or a frozen Hershey's Kiss.

♡ Get a package of mint-flavored condoms. You can order them from a catalog or get them at many variety stores. Silly but fun.

♡ Suck a peppermint candy or use a very minty mouthwash before making love. It also makes oral sex feel that much spicier.

Saturday Night # 10

Erotic Beginnings
—Part I

$\mathcal{E}$rotic dreams. Sexual fantasies. Like everyone else in the world, you probably have at least one, an image that pops into your mind in the middle of the night that makes you feel sexy. Fantasies form the basis of most romance novels, movies, and TV shows.

In our sexual fantasies, we're nineteen, gorgeous or handsome, sexy as hell, with a well-developed body that everyone envies. We never have to worry about disease or anything unexpected happening, because it's our dream and we can chart the course. When I was in my teens, my fantasies revolved around those gorgeous guys on the Ponderosa: the Cartwrights. The image of those men can still make my heart beat just a bit faster, even in reruns. Later it was some tall, dark, and incredibly sexy guy I saw across a restaurant, who would want only me and carry me off to his lair. Okay. You get the picture.

What do you do in those fantasies? Anything. Absolutely anything. Things you might actually want to do, things you wouldn't even consider. But then you don't have to apologize for what you dream. There's no such thing as a bad fantasy. Only actions can be bad.

Have you ever shared your fantasy? Probably not. You feel it's too personal, too dangerous to share. He'll never understand. She'll think I'm perverted. He'll laugh. She'll be shocked. Well, probably none of those things are totally true, but, of course, you don't have to share unless you want to.

There are some classic fantasies that many of us have. For this Saturday night, I've written the beginning of a few for you and your partner to share. You'll probably be able to find at least one you've secretly enjoyed in one form or another. Read it alone or with your partner. Change the names and descriptions of the characters to match your own if you like, or leave the participants undescribed, living purely in your dreams.

Sort out whether this might be a fantasy you two might want to act out or just one that's fun to think and dream about. If you want to act it out, that's not difficult. Use the dialogue and each take a role. Expand, excite, explore. Pick up the story where I end it and continue it into unexplored realms. Play!

HORSEBACK

She was riding along the beach, enjoying the feel of the wind flowing through her long coal black hair. The force of it pressed her soft white silk blouse against her body, clearly outlining her large breasts. She could feel the play of the horse's powerful muscles against the insides of her thighs and hear the loud thudding of his hooves. A large wave splashed onto the beach and the spindrift splashed as the pair galloped along.

She was disappointed to see a rider approaching from the other direction, interrupting her delicious solitude. She slowed her mount, then stopped and gazed at him. As he drew closer, she made our details: the midnight black mount he rode with athletic skill and grace, the dark shirt and pants he wore, his ebony hair blowing in the breeze, his long, powerful fingers holding the reins. All combined to create the image of a marauding warrior. She could almost imagine a mask over his face. Somehow, she knew that he was dangerous and she should turn her mount and gallop away. But she didn't, couldn't.

Maybe he'll just ride by, she thought, feeling a tightening low in her belly. But his dark eyes were on her, roaming her body in a way that should have terrified her. But all his gaze did was feed the fire inside of her.

He closed the distance between them and reined in his horse, pulling the beast up so that he reared and pawed the air. Frightened, her mount shied and neighed loudly. As she controlled her horse, the man moved so the two beasts were head-to-tail and he was only a breath away from her. His thigh pressed against hers and she could feel the heat of his body through their clothing. Run, she told herself. This is a man with whom you could lose your head and your heart. Yet still she stayed, gazing into his fathomless eyes.

When the animals quieted, he said, "I had to stop, you know. I had to see you, touch you." He reached out and cupped her chin.

And she did know. "Yes," she whispered.

He wrapped his powerful arm around her waist and pulled her close. She braced her palms against the flat strength of his chest, feeling his heart pound as quickly as hers.

"I want you," he growled, his voice almost mesmerizing as it echoed through her soul as though it had always been there. She knew she should stop him, but she was powerless against the pull of whatever entwined them. "I'm confused," she whispered.

45

"I know, but don't be. I would never harm you, but I just have to . . ."

Have to what? she thought. But she knew. She knew how this encounter was going to progress and she knew she should be scared. But she wasn't. She closed her eyes and took a deep breath, testing whether it would clear her head and bring back her ability to reason. It did not, and she didn't care. She knew only that she wanted whatever was going to happen.

"I'm leaving in the morning, so we only have tonight," he said, his lips brushing hers.

"Yes," she whispered, "we have tonight."

Their lips met, his strong and powerful, hers soft and yielding. His tongue invaded her mouth, possessing her. His teeth nipped at her lower lip, teasing and taking, yet giving, too. His hand slid lower, cupping her buttocks, and her body answered. She rose in the stirrups, fighting to get closer to the warmth of him.

"Come with me," he said, and she could feel the warmth of his breath against her mouth.

"Yes," she said, and together they rode down the beach.

On the Water

The air was warm on Barb's face as the small sailboat glided slowly across the lake. Her husband, Paul, had the sails closely trimmed, so the boat moved at a leisurely pace on the mirrorlike water. "How about we anchor and share something to eat?" he called out.

Barb yelled her agreement, then readied the anchor. The boat slowed, then finally stopped, rocking slightly in the middle of the lake, at some distance from the other small boats out for the afternoon. "I brought a surprise," Paul said as Barb threw the anchor overboard and felt it catch on the bottom.

"Really?"

Paul fumbled in a cooler and brought out a bottle of champagne. "Great," Barb said as she got the paper cups. "Wonderful idea." She found the cheese and crackers she had packed, and together they talked and enjoyed their treats. As time passed, Barb felt herself a bit tipsy. "What a fantastic day."

"You're fantastic, too," Paul said, sliding over close to his wife. He draped his arm around her shoulders and kissed her gently on the lips.

"Don't get too amorous, lover boy," Barb said, giggling. "We're here in the middle of the lake."

"And?"

"And . . . don't be silly. We can't make love here. Someone will see."

Paul pulled his wife onto the deck of the small sailboat. "The other boats are too far away for anyone to see anything." He slipped his hand beneath Barb's tank top and found the hook to her bra. "Anyway, it's kind of kinky, knowing someone just might see us."

Barb protested mildly, but knew she'd give in. It is kind of kinky, she thought. She felt the warmth of the sun on her nipples as Paul slipped off her bra.

Sometimes in our fantasies, we're shy, and someone overcomes our reluctance and takes charge.

A Pickup

He sat at the end of the bar, nursing his scotch and soda, looking at the attractive woman sitting with her legs crossed beneath her short skirt. She wore a red blouse with long, loose sleeves and white pearl buttons. Her blouse was unbuttoned far

47

enough to show more than a hint of well-shaped breasts. He looked at her long red fingernails and fantasized about how they would feel raking across his body. She glanced at him, then continued her animated conversation with the bartender. Her face glowed as she laughed in response to something that the bartender said to her.

Should I offer to buy her a drink? he wondered. When she looked at him, her glance seemed neither inviting nor hostile. He had no clue whether she would welcome an advance or politely tell him to get lost. Shit, he thought, women have it so easy. All they have to do is sit there and look pretty. Men approach *them.* They never have to risk being rejected. And what should I say to her? Do you come here often? Hot day today, isn't it? What's your sign? That's a beautiful blouse you're wearing, but I'd like to rip it off you?

Although he was lonely and felt drawn to the woman, he decided to finish his drink and go home. Sometimes it just isn't worth the hassle, he thought. Even if she agreed to have a drink with him, he would have to play the game—small talk, flattery— the usual preliminaries to getting laid. It just seemed like too much work.

He turned away with a sigh, downed the last of his drink, and began to scoop some of his change off the bar. Then he heard a voice behind him. "Are you leaving so soon?"

He swung around on the bar stool and found himself face-to-face with the woman. She was looking directly into his eyes and smiling. "Uh, yeah. I mean . . . no," he stammered, unable to think of what to say, feeling like a complete fool.

"Oh, good, " she said. "Would you like some company?"

"I sure would," he replied. "Do you come here often?"

"No, I don't, and you really don't have to use lines like that with me."

He was completely at a loss on how to respond to this situation, so he simply said, "Yeah, well I never know what to say when I'm trying to pick up a woman."

"But you're not trying to pick me up. I'm trying to pick you up, so why don't you just relax."

"You are?" he asked. Oh God, I must sound like a complete fool, he thought.

Her face lit up as she laughed. Her laugh was so spontaneous and bright that he knew she wasn't laughing at him. "Well, I'm at least considering it," she replied. "You were looking at me before, weren't you?"

"I'm sorry," he replied, "I didn't mean to stare or make you feel uncomfortable."

"You weren't staring, and you didn't make me feel uncomfortable. You made me feel sexy. I was watching you, too. You seemed lonely and I was attracted to you. And you were looking at me as if you wanted to tear my blouse off. Is that what you were thinking?" She smiled and looked into his eyes.

"Uh, yeah. And I was imagining how your beautiful fingernails would feel raking across my naked body," he said, surprising himself.

"I like that in a man." She laughed. Then she lifted her hand and lightly stroked his face with her nails. "Does that feel good?" she asked.

He shuddered with pleasure, then gently took her hand in his, drew it to his mouth, and licked the spaces between her fingers.

She leaned toward him and whispered into his ear. "I'm only in town for a few days and I'm staying at the hotel just around the corner. Why don't we have a drink or two and get to know each other a little and then maybe we can decide what to do about those wonderful fantasies of yours?"

He ordered another round of drinks. Tonight is going to be a night to remember, he thought.

49

*   *   *

Were you able to use these tales? If nothing here matched one of your fantasies, create another. Or skip ahead to Saturday Night #25 for the next group of fantasy beginnings.

Saturday Night # 11

Erotic Mall Walking

$\mathcal{T}$onight, let's take a walk around the local mall. Not a sexual activity, you say. It is when you use your creative mind and think in new and sexy ways about what you find in the stores. So wander, look at things with a new perspective, giggle and whisper with your partner. It will warm you both up, and it's also a great way to subtly suggest a game for another Saturday.

The Drugstore

Drugstores don't just sell drugs anymore, so walk around with your thoughts turned to the bedroom. How would your tongue feel on your partner's body after you've sucked on a menthol cough drop? How about buying a bottle of "magic" sugar pills and agreeing that whoever takes one becomes the sex

51

slave of the other? How about a makeup assortment to change your image completely, or some scented soap that's completely different from what you use now?

Maybe you could buy some adhesive tape and put a long strip on your partner's body, then rip it off as orgasm approaches. See those chemical, flexible, freezable, heatable ice/heat packs for athletes? What parts of his or her anatomy might you heat- or cold-wrap?

The Kitchen/Bathroom Store

How about that satin pillowcase? How would a stack of pillows covered in satin look and feel beneath your partner's knees or buttocks while you make love? If you covered your lover's head with a pillowcase, it would act like a lightweight, less threatening blindfold. Maybe you could watch your partner shower through a transparent shower curtain. If she held one of those small decorative soaps between her knees while you made love, it would create a tight channel for your penis.

The Shoe Store

Those ridiculously high-heeled knee-high boots might create a new mood in the bedroom. A pair of knee-high stockings worn on your hands gives caresses a new feel. The scent of leather might turn one of you on and might lead to some interesting revelations.

The Toy Store

No, not that kind of toy store, but a real kiddie place. How about that really fuzzy stuffed animal? Wouldn't it feel wonderful rubbed softly on your partner's back? What about winding up a toy and letting it walk up your partner's bare chest? What part of your partner's body would you caress with those soft paintbrushes? His testicles? Her nipples?

The Hardware Area of the Department Store

See that bunch of ladders leaning against the wall? What would happen if your lover climbed one without any underwear on? For a new sensation, how about rubbing some part of your partner's body very lightly with a small piece of sandpaper.

We'll investigate bondage games on another Saturday night, but for now, just consider what you might do with a fifty-foot piece of soft nylon rope or several long bungee cords. And what about that length of heavy chain? Wouldn't if feel good just draped over your naked body? Or your partner's? Over there is a display of various-sized padlocks and there are some clothespins. Hmm . . .

The Boutique

What outrageous things do you think you two might do if one of you was dressed in something totally different? How about a peasant blouse and full skirt? A tight leather miniskirt? A bikini top only? A pair of satin shorts? A thong? Maybe those earrings that look like chandeliers, or that multistrand necklace? How about wearing a pair of mirrored sunglasses so you can look wherever you please?

The Video Store

Some of the most arousing videos aren't the X-rated kind.

Think about the sexiest scene you've ever watched. Would it be Sharon Stone being interrogated by Michael Douglas in *Basic Instinct*? Kirk Douglas pressing Kim Novak against a tree and pushing his knee between her legs in *Strangers When We Meet*? The great scene beside the railroad tracks in *Picnic* or the dance in the same film? The love scenes in *Titanic* or *Shakespeare in Love*? Discuss scenes like these in detail, then rent a film and do what they do.

A workout video takes on a whole new dimension when you exercise together naked. Maybe he does push-ups, with her beneath.

The Stationery Store

Look at those scissors. Wouldn't they work well to cut holes in an old sweatshirt or sweatpants? Then you could tease your partner with just hints of what lies beneath. What erotic things could you do to your body or your partner's with paper clips, rubber bands, or mucilage? And all that paint! You don't have to do them, remember, just talk about them.

The Food Court

What could you spread over your body, or your partner's, to encourage licking and sucking? The only limit is your imagination.

The Sporting Goods Store

What could you two do on that weight bench? It's just the right height, isn't it? Wouldn't she look sexy in that tight spandex workout suit? Picture him wearing those formfitting latex bicycle shorts and nothing else. What would happen if you used your

hands and made your partner climax without taking the tight clothing off?

The Greeting Card Store

My friends and I used to play a game when I was quite young. We'd create "dirty" sayings by adding the words *between the sheets* to song titles. It works just as well with the soppy sayings on greeting cards: Wish you were here; good luck; congratulations. Think about the card you would write if your partner was far away. What would you say about how you spend your late nights?

And what creative things might you do with gift wrap, ribbons, and bows? What might you wrap with flexible foil or tissue paper?

I think you get the idea. Wander tonight, first with your feet, then with your mind. You don't actually have to buy anything. The object of tonight is to open your mind and exercise the most erogenous zone of all, your imagination, then share all your deliciously erotic thoughts with your partner.

Saturday Night #12

Eroticism: A Game of Sensations

P laying with all of your senses makes sex more varied and thus more fun. That's the focus of this evening's activity.

Like what?

THE SENSE OF TOUCH

Heat and Cold

Stroke you partner's body with an ice cube or just hold one in your mouth as you kiss. Once your mouth is cold, use your freezing tongue to lick all those luscious spots.

For Her

❤♡ Keep that ice cube in your mouth as you lick the end of his penis. It's a sensation that's nearly irresistible.

For Him

❤♡ Slide an ice cube into her vaginal passage. It's not as jarring as you might think, and the feel of the melting water trickling out is really great.

For Both of You

❤♡ I'm told that a tiny bit of Ben-Gay on the tip of the penis gives a tingling sensation. And one visitor to my Web site wrote that she enjoyed having a bit of a jalapeño pepper rubbed on her vaginal tissues. Hmm. I'm not really sure about that one, but I pass it along for fun. With anything that you're going to rub on your body, please beware of nasty reactions. And only use things that are water-soluble, so they can be quickly removed if worse comes to worst.

Here's one for the bravest souls. Hot wax can be really sexy when dripped onto your partner's arms, thighs, or buttocks. Yes, really. And it's not sadistic, just tantalizing. Take care with the candle, using a tip-proof holder, and hold it high above the skin. Wax cools very quickly, so the farther from your skin it's held, the cooler the wax is when it makes contact. Be sure to try it on yourself first so you know just how far from the skin it must be held for the proper sensation.

Rough and Smooth

Use a piece of fur to stroke your partner's body. You might have an old winter glove with a furry lining or the collar off of an old coat. If you haven't any fur, try some satin or silk. You can get a piece at any fabric store. Stroke erotic areas slowly with the cool, smooth material.

Sometimes you can find an old pair of satin gloves at a garage sale. Put them on and caress your partner. Or use the latex gloves that doctors use. You can get them at most drugstores.

Then switch to something quite rough, like a piece of burlap or canvas, even a piece of emery board or light sandpaper. Don't get too aggressive, just light touches. But make sure your partner feels it.

For Him

❤️ If you've got a case of five o'clock shadow, use your rough cheek to gently rub the insides of her thighs or the backs of her knees.

For Both of You

❤️ Use your teeth, lightly, to cause just a hint of pain, not to hurt, mind you, just to increase the sensations. If this seems to raise the heat, here's an adventure to try. Just as you are about to climax, slap your partner once, lightly, on the buttocks. Cup your hand so the contact is more noise than feeling. It can be deeply erotic. Later, ask your partner whether he or she liked it and guide yourself accordingly.

Revel in the sensations of making love. Spend a lovemaking session using only the tips of your fingers. Or sit cross-legged opposite each other, close your eyes, and touch. Just touch—all over.

For Fun

❤♡ Brush your partner's hair with a coarse brush. It feels wonderful and awakens the skin everywhere.

THE SENSE OF SMELL

Wonderful aromas can trigger good feelings and wonderful memories more than any other sense. Use a new perfume or aftershave. Change the smell of the bedroom with a scented candle or a stick or cone of incense. Many find that vanilla is an erotic aroma. I just think of baking cookies, but see what appeals to you.

There are dozens of books on aromatherapy that advocate the use of scent burners to perfume the bedroom. Neroli or jasmine, lavender or bergamot—experiment with different essential oils to see what brings out the sensualist in both of you. And don't overlook a few drops of essential oil in your bath or on a cotton ball to scent your lingerie.

Erotic smells don't have to be sweet. The odor of clean sweat can be arousing. In some cultures, a handkerchief worn next to the body during dancing is used to arouse a partner. A person can be sexiest after strenuous exercise, hot and slippery and smelling of hard work. You might also enjoy the smell of your partner right after a hot shower.

59

THE SOUNDS OF LOVE

For another Saturday night, we'll talk at length about playing old records, so I'll just give it a mention here. Remember the song that was playing the first time you made love? Enough said. Want to put on Ravel's *Bolero*? Go for it. Just be sure that you're not making love to a rerun of *The Lucy Show*.

Recently, I found a rack containing tapes of nature's sounds in my local discount store. They had cassettes containing the songs of whales and the sounds of the pounding surf, wolves calling in the night, and the wind in pine trees, among others. If you've ever spent a weekend in a mountain cabin or a cottage by the sea, maybe one of these tapes can help to re-create a magical moment. Or create the sounds of a summer evening during the winter.

Have you ever used those wonderfully naughty four-letter words while making love? You might find that a juicy, very explicit noun or verb, whispered at just the right moment, can drive your partner crazy. Do you want to take this a step further? If your partner has never used such language, teasing and "forcing" your lover to voice his or her exact desires in four-letter detail can lead to really hot times. Many years ago, I was about to climax, when a partner demanded that I tell him where I wanted him to put his penis. I had never used words like *pussy* so it caught me by surprise. The time it took me to finally state what I needed was agonizing and incredibly erotic.

THE LOOK OF LOVE

Don't overlook the romantic power of candles. Not just one but a dozen, filling the bedroom with romantic shadows. Or light an old oil lamp or make love in the glow of a fire in the fireplace.

Overdone? Maybe, but like most women, I'm a sucker for mood lighting, and it's a marvelous way to tell your partner, Tonight I want to make long, passionate love to you. What a wonderful message to send.

Want to use the sense of sight to tease? Take some old clothes and cut holes in strategic places so that your partner gets just a hint of the body beneath.

For Her

❤♡ Cut an old top so short that it barely covers your breasts. Or cut holes at the front of an old bra; then wear something almost transparent.

For Him

❤♡ Leave your jeans unfastened so they form that sexy vee that women like to explore. And go barefoot.

Whatever you do, appeal to all the senses to envelop your partner in lovemaking.

Saturday Night # 13

Being a New Lover

What kind of lover are you? It's always difficult to see ourselves objectively, but try for this week to see what kind of lover you are. Are you aggressive? Passive? Tender? A bit rough? Do you make the first move or do you respond to your partner?

We all fall into patterns of behavior, and how you act in the bedroom is certainly no exception. I'll bet that sex usually begins with the same signals. Who sends the signals, you or your partner? Is that signal subtle: a raised eyebrow or a special caress? Is it overt: a passionate kiss or a grab under the covers?

Take some time and think about what kind of lover you are. Then, for tonight, be someone different.

Are you the passive, shy type? Do you wait until your lover makes the first move? Tonight, you make that move. It might be as simple as turning down the lights in the bedroom or wearing a sexy, inviting outfit. Or wearing nothing at all.

Want to be more aggressive? Rent an erotic video and have it playing on the VCR when your partner arrives in the bedroom. Grab your partner's wrist and growl, "Your side of the bed or mine?" If it feels a bit odd, that's fine, too. You're telling your partner, I'm in the mood. Let's fool around. What could be nicer? If you have the urge to giggle, that's just fine. Laughter should be a wonderful part of bedroom play.

Are you usually the aggressor? Tonight, be shy. Invite with your eyes, not with your voice. Suggest with a subtle stroke or a gentle whisper, but make your partner ask you.

Another way to change your behavior in the bedroom is to consider the kind of a lover you wish your partner was. That can form a template for the way you act and react. If you wish he was more tender, be tender and show him how you would like to feel. If you wish she was more passionate, be more passionate, yourself, demonstrating your desires the way you wish she would.

For Her

♥♡Spend the evening in something tight and short, with a tight tank top and no bra. Got high heels and black stockings with seams up the back? Add a garter belt and you're ready for some different styles of loving. Are you a woman who wears a business suit all day? How about a peasant blouse with a full skirt and no undies? Have you got some big junky jewelry, dark red lipstick, daring perfume? And forget the blow-dryer for one evening. Leave your hair natural, fluffy or straight, and let him run his fingers through it. If you've got long hair, how about putting it up with one barrette so you can let it down later with a flourish?

63

For Him

♥♡ If you're the business type, how about a biker outfit, with tight jeans, a leather jacket, and heavy boots? Maybe you have nothing on under the jacket or the pants. Wear a pair of sexy shorts in the middle of the winter. Does she like to undress you? You might want to wear something really complicated or have a surprise pair of tight Speedo trunks on under your slacks.

For Fun

♥♡ Stay in your business clothes and allow your partner to mess you up. Let her peel off your tie or urge him to pull the pins from your hair. Remember Kim Novak urging Jimmy Stewart to "muss me a little" in *Vertigo*?

I think you've got the idea. Whatever you do this evening, break the mold and be someone new, exciting, and different.

The End of the First Quarter

I t's the end of your first thirteen weeks, and I hope that most of you are beginning to get a little more comfortable with lovemaking. You and your partner have taken the first baby steps toward better communication and you've both discovered that the rewards are well worth the risks. You've made a few booboos and had a few laughs, but that's normal and delightful.

A few of you are reading this book but haven't gotten up the courage to share your thoughts and desires with your partner. It's never too early to begin, so take that first step. You and your partner will be incredibly glad you did.

In the next quarter, we'll venture further into the world of sexual fantasies and begin a journey on the Internet. Okay, let's go on to more adventurous Saturday nights.

Saturday Night # 14

Variety Is the Spice

I remember being about ten years old and getting ahold of a magazine that described sexual positions. I had a wonderful relationship with my mother, so I asked her which position she and my father had used when they conceived me. After she stopped laughing, my mother explained that loving couples have intercourse often and that while making love, they move from one position to another. I was amazed and a bit puzzled. I wondered why anyone would want to do such an awkward thing for any reason other than making babies. Okay, don't laugh at my ignorance. Remember, this was in the early fifties, before Jerry Springer.

In the years that followed, of course, I learned—a lot. The positions that you get into with your partner during sex are really a very personal thing, and they can be quite varied. They flow naturally from one to another as you move and turn to increase or change the sensations. However, many people fall into patterns that become routine. Be it the missionary position or something a bit more creative, I have the feeling that you usually "do it" in the same way. How about doing things differently tonight?

The term *missionary position* came about because Christian missionaries believed that "man on top" was the only acceptable position. They felt that other positions were "animal" and to be shunned. Of course in those days, women frequently made love with their nightclothes on. What more is there to say?

There's nothing wrong with the missionary position. It's satisfying and comfortable for most people, and it allows the man's hands access to the woman's breasts. It's great for being able to see and kiss each other, and she can stroke his chest, buttocks, and back while making love. She can also stroke herself or wrap her legs around the man's waist to deepen the sensation. This is also one of the best positions for conception, if that's your desire.

Drawbacks: It's difficult for the man to reach the woman's clitoris and for her to reach his testicles to add those touches to the mix. In addition, a woman may find that the weight of a man on her body limits the movements of her pelvis.

If you enjoy the missionary position, you might try having the woman put her legs over the man's shoulders. It's a delicious change, further deepening the penetration and allowing him to manually stimulate her clitoris.

Making love with the woman on top is usually accomplished by the man lying on his back while the woman crouches on her knees, then straddles, mounts, and rides him. It's particularly good for a woman who wants more control of the speed and depth of penetration. It leaves both partners' hands free for touching, as well. During lovemaking, the woman can straighten her legs or even turn so she's facing his feet to adjust the angle of penetration. This position can be good for the final months of pregnancy, when putting pressure on a woman's abdomen is uncomfortable for her.

Drawbacks: It's more difficult for a woman to become pregnant this way, since semen tends to flow out of her vagina. In addition, if the man has problems maintaining an erection, his penis might fall out of her body, which can be quite frustrating. Some women also find that penetration can be too deep this way.

The two partners can lie side by side, facing each other. A couple can begin this way or, when either the man or the woman is on top, roll over to it. It's hard to get deep penetration this way, but kissing and fondling are a natural.

Rear entry is sometimes called "doggie-style." In this case I don't refer to anal sex, but to entering a woman's vagina from behind her. There are several ways to accomplish this. The woman can get on her knees or she can kneel beside a bed or chair, with the upper part of her body on the horizontal surface. She can also lean over a table or countertop. Then the man can guide his penis in gently and hold the woman's hips to control the thrusting. In this position, it's difficult for her to touch him, but he can reach around and caress her breasts or clitoris.

Drawbacks: Rear entry prevents any stimulation of the clitoris except with the hands, and it's difficult to kiss or even see your partner's face. This lack of intimacy makes it less desirable for some couples.

If you want to experiment with this position, please take special care not to spread anything from the anus to the vagina. If the tip of the penis touches the anal area, clean it well before vaginal penetration. If you're using a condom, change it before intercourse. Anal bacteria can lead to nasty vaginal infections.

With the man seated on a chair, the woman can sit on his lap, guiding his erect penis into her. She can sit either facing toward or away from him. Facing each other lends itself to kissing, her breasts are at mouth height, and both people's hands are free to roam.

Drawbacks: This position is probably the worst in terms of depth of penetration, and if he has a problem maintaining an erection, it can be difficult for his penis to remain inside.

I've seen couples making love standing up in films and have

read about it in books. I've never, however, made it work. Maybe the men I've tried it with weren't strong enough to support me, but however we tried, someone always either slipped or cramped a muscle. But there are those, I'm sure, who can do it. With the woman's back pressed against a wall (or a tree, like in the films), she wraps her legs around his waist and he enters her this way. If he's really strong, he can support her entire weight and carry her around. It seems a good way for deep penetration, but those of you with weak backs, take care.

For Her

❤️ Gather several pillows, large and small, and experiment. Try having him kneel on several beside the bed while you lie back across the bed, your legs on his shoulders. Or place a few beneath his buttocks during intercourse.

For Him

❤️ How about having her climb on your lap, facing you, her legs around your waist? It might be even more delightful if you are fully clothed, with your zipper open, of course, and she is wearing a full skirt and no undies.

For Fun

❤️ Here's a particularly interesting position. He lies on his side and she on her back, perpendicular to him, her legs over his hips. Thus his penis has direct access to her vagina and both partners' hands are free to play.

For Him

♥♡ Here's a great tease. In whatever position, enter her just an inch or so. Then ask, "Want more? Say *please*." Making it last this way is erotic torture and increases the sexual tension that much more.

If you read the *Kama Sutra,* you'll find that there are many other positions detailed. Any and all are valid, although some of the ones I've seen seem physically impossible.

Remember, change can be exciting, so do it differently tonight. The point is, variety is the spice of sex, so play and experiment to your heart's, and body's, content.

For Fun

♥♡ During sex, we all tend to find a comfortable position and stay there. Tonight, try stopping intercourse several times and changing positions. This allows experimentation with lots of different arrangements, but, more important, the stopping, separating, and then starting again increases the tension with each adjustment. You will find yourselves getting even more aroused than usual.

For Fun

♥♡ Try writing the details of several positions on slips of paper and drawing one out of a hat. Then, you have to end the night in that position.

Saturday Night # 15

Talking Romance

*H*ave you ever wanted to seduce your partner verbally? It's such an integral part of so many romance novels. It's usually the handsome hero who whispers to the beautiful heroine, telling her how he'd like to make love to her. He sets the scene, painting exotic word pictures. You can do it, too, whether you're male or female. Let me give you several images to help you set the scene tonight. I'm sure at least one will work for you.

Before you begin, try to make your voice more seductive. Lower the pitch and reduce the volume. You're not trying to reach the rafters here, so speak softly. Relax your shoulders and take deep breaths. Let your voice become a bit breathier—go for that Marilyn Monroe sound.

Here, you'll find lots of settings for your story of love. Sit together on the sofa in front of a fire, lie on a blanket in the yard and look up at the stars, or cuddle in bed, holding each other. Make a cassette of your tale and put it in your partner's car tape deck. Whisper a short story as you pause together in the hallway. Tell your partner how you two will make magic together. "This is how I'd love to make love to you." Continue the scene for as long as you like, until it's time to make it real.

FIRELIGHT

We are in a large living room that's filled with soft furniture, large pillows, and a fluffy carpet. The room has a giant fireplace and I start a huge roaring fire, then turn out all the lights. The room is cool, so the fire warms one side of our bodies while the rest is still chilled. The room smells of wood smoke and we can hear the crackling of the logs. Occasionally, one piece of flaming wood breaks and falls, releasing a spray of sparks. They come close to us but never touch our skin.

We lie together on the thick furry rug and I dip strawberries in chocolate sauce and feed them to you one at a time. You get some chocolate on your lips and I lick it off with the tip of my tongue. Our lips meet in a long, drugging kiss.

THE HOT SUN

We are walking on a beach late in the afternoon. The sun is setting, but the sand is warm beneath our feet. You're wearing a bathing suit, still wet from our swim in the cool surf. We wander along the soft sand, but soon the bottoms of our feet get too hot and we move to the edge of the sea, letting the waves lap at our ankles.

There's no one else on the beach, but we don't even wonder why. Gulls wheel and cry overhead, splash into the waves from time to time, then climb into the air with a free meal. As the sun lowers in the sky, a soft, cool breeze springs up. Our steps slow until we stand, facing each other, taking in all the tiny details of each other's loving looks. We don't know who moves, but we are soon in each other's arms. I kiss you so softly, just a brush of my lips on yours.

MASQUERADE

We are at a masquerade party, our faces concealed behind large dominoes. We meet beside the door to the patio and our gazes lock, our eyes saying so much that words aren't necessary. I open the glass door and we step outside. The night is warm, the breeze soft and gentle, smelling of magnolias and jasmine. I touch your hair, so fine and silken, and I feel you shiver. We realize that we haven't said a word, yet our silence speaks volumes.

I slip my fingertips over your throat, feeling the beating of your pulse. I know as I touch that it is speeding up, as mine is. I see your lips part, hear your breathing quicken, and know that although later we'll be together, I will never know your real identity. But I don't care. I just know that I have to have you.

SUNSET

We are standing on top of a mountain, leaning on rocks still warm from the heat of the day. The molten red sun slides toward the horizon, creating streaks of gold and orange across the sky. I slip my arm around your waist, holding you close as the world seems to pause at the end of the day.

Until a moment ago, birds have been singing, but now they are silent, holding their breath as the day slowly surrenders to the night. The wind calms, and we can hear the sounds of each other's breathing and our soft sighs as the colors blend and deepen.

The sun's only half a disk now as I begin to stroke your back. You know how much I want you, how gently I will take you later in the tent we've pitched for the night. Yet you also know that we have all the time in the world. We are patient.

I'm sure you have your own picture of some romantic spot to make love. Let yourself go. Create the scene. Appeal to all the senses. Move slowly, savoring every minute.

Will you feel a little strange telling these stories to your lover? Maybe. So what?

Saturday Night # 16

The Good Old Days

Most of us remember with tenderness and a smile the good things in the history of a relationship. Put this to work for a Saturday evening to remember.

For Either of You

♥ Take some time and plan a re-creation of a wonderful evening from your past together. Maybe the first night you made love or an afternoon at the beach or park. Think it all through and rebuild as many pieces of that date as you can.

Remember an evening you spent in your house alone while you were dating. Your parents were out for the evening, or maybe you had your own apartment. Build on that. Did you go out for dinner first? Make reservations at the same place. Did you eat in? Try to remember what you had for dinner and make the same menu. TV dinners? Steak and asparagus? It doesn't matter. Did you have wine? Beer? A fancy blender concoction? Have the same drink ingredients on hand.

What music was playing? Select anything from Sinatra to Springsteen to Sondheim to Stravinsky. Whatever curls your toes. But try to keep your selections romantic and easy to listen to. If you insist on rap music, I guess that's fine, but not as conducive to loving as Michael Bolton or Natalie Cole, in my opinion.

Do you remember the scent you were using? Odors bring back memories much more vividly than any other sense. I still flash back to an old boyfriend whenever I smell Old Spice. Maybe you used to chew gum. Get some of the same kind so that your breath will smell as it once did. (But please, don't make noise when you chew. That can ruin the mood!)

What were you wearing? Can you find some clothes similar to those? If it wasn't too long ago, you might just find the old outfit in the back of your closet. If it's been a long time since that evening, you might have to get a bit creative with the wardrobe. If you have some time, visit a few garage or rummage sales. They might have just what you're looking for.

Did you do some slow dancing? I just love body rubbing, and that's really all slow dancing is. Guys, I know dancing probably isn't your thing. It seems awkward and you feel ridiculous. But remember, you don't have to be good at it. Just stand in the center of the room, hold her against your body, and shuffle your feet. It doesn't matter how, just move them. And move your hands. Stroke the sides of her breasts the way you did when you tried to touch what's-her-name's body in high school.

Recently, one of our local radio stations was playing the top five hundred oldies of all time. When I heard "Earth Angel" by the Penguins, a particular favorite from my past, I asked Ed to dance, and we did. Well, actually, our feet hardly moved, but our bodies rubbed really nicely. It's wonderful how interesting parts stick out so that they rub against your partner's interesting parts. Anyway, by the end of "In the Still of the Night" by the Five Satins, we were half undressed and . . . well, I needn't go any further. It was a terrific evening indeed.

Maybe you remember a picnic. Plan another trip to the same spot, if you can mange it. Prepare similar foods, maybe those messy ones that caused you two to lick each other's fingers and then move on to other parts. Take a very large blanket, as well as a lighter one. When you get there, clear the area where you're going to lie of branches and rocks. There's nothing less conducive to long lovemaking than trying to fool around on a blanket and discovering every stone and stick with your naked back. So you can guard your privacy, use the second blanket to cover both of you if you plan to make love out-of-doors. For some, the thrill of possibly being discovered adds to the excitement. For others, it's more appropriate to neck on the blanket and reserve the lovemaking for the bedroom.

How about creating this picnic in the living room beside a roaring fire? There's much more privacy there, and you can make love right on the rug. Take care if you do, however, to lie on a blanket or towel to avoid a painful backside in the morning. Take advice from one who's actually made love this way and had nasty rug burns on the base of her spine the next day.

The key to this evening, as with all others, is to have fun together and make the effort to do something unpredictable.

A word of advice: If your spouse creates such an evening, go along with the plan. Don't get all stuffy and serious. Your partner has gone to quite a bit of trouble to plan it, so go with the flow. It will end up being beautiful, I promise. Beware. If you stomp on your partner's creative impulses now, it might be quite awhile before you get another chance to play together, if you ever do. If you might have done something differently, do it your way next week. Another wonderful evening? What a great idea.

For Fun

❤♡Here's another idea. Do you remember necking in the car? It's not as ridiculous as you might think. Invite your partner out for an evening. Go to a movie or visit some friends. Afterward, drive to that special spot and park. Put some soft music on the radio and neck the way you did back then. Kiss, touch, rub, and let the feeling build. If the necessary gymnastics to make love in the front seat of your Honda seem a bit much, drive home and finish the evening in the bedroom. If, however, you feel particularly adventurous, consummate it right there. But if you really want to do it in the car, take care to ensure your privacy. Doing it in your car in your own driveway or even in the garage can seem weird, but it's safe from prying eyes or police with flashlights. Quite a few evenings were ruined for me by such an invasion.

One final word: If you want to make love in a car, just be sure to turn the engine off or open a window slightly.

For Fun

❤♡Rummage through all your old records, select the most meaningful ones, and create a tape or recordable CD. If you've got a system with a microphone, you can add your comments between selections—for example, "Do you remember the night we danced to this at the senior prom?" Ed made such a tape for me, and I still cherish it. I can play it when we're not together to evoke all the loving thoughts I have of him.

Saturday Night #17

Afterglow

Too many couples turn away and fall asleep as soon as the sex is over. Tonight, we're going to turn our attention to the afterglow, that magical time after a wonderful interlude of lovemaking. That's the time to say a few words about sex—very few.

Now's a good time to tell your partner what was wonderful, and be specific. "I loved it when you . . ." Remember, if he or she has done something different, your partner will be unsure as to whether it was okay. Help out. Tell your partner how much you enjoyed it. Use lots of words and gestures. Kiss, hug, and cuddle while you discuss it.

If your partner isn't talking, you might ask whether there was anything that he or she would change. "Was it okay that I . . . ?" Ed and I do that frequently, especially after a new or long-forgotten activity. I remember the first time he slapped my bottom as I climaxed. He thought I would enjoy it, and I did. The small shock was just what I needed to drive me over the edge. Although I thought I had made it clear that I had enjoyed it, afterward he remained unsure. I was oblivious to his troubles.

It took quite awhile for him to share his doubts. I was almost asleep when he whispered, "Was it all right when I slapped you?" We spent awhile talking and eventually he was content. Now, however, we try to be more conscious of each other's doubts. Sometimes each of us needs reassurance that what we've done is really okay. Ask. It takes a lot of the pressure off.

Did you think of some erotic activity during sex but didn't try it? Well, afterward is the opportunity to mention it. "You know, while we were making love, I thought about doing . . . It sounded really hot to me. Do you think you might have liked that?"

I hesitate to give you so many things to talk about afterward. Take care not to dissect the evening's fun and games ad nauseam. One or two sentences before falling asleep can be enough. More next time.

And whatever you did together, be sure to cuddle. That afterward time can be the most intimate of all, so hold each other. Sharing this time of intimacy can go a long way to smoothing over the frustrations of the day. Small aggravations are forgotten in the warm cocoon you two share. You both can fall asleep gently, with the sexiness held close against your skin.

Stroke your lover and encourage him or her to touch you. If your partner tends to roll over and go to sleep, suggest that you'd like to hold and be held. At a moment like this, hinting probably won't work. Both of you are a bit muddled, so ask for what you want. Be specific. Whisper, "Um, sweetheart, put your arms around me." Snuggle up and say softly, "I love the feeling of your naked body against mine, so don't leave just yet."

You might even awake to more fun and games.

For Fun

❤♡ One of the most delicious things that Ed and I have ever done after sex is for one of us to go into the bathroom, get a warm, wet cloth, and then wash each other. Sex is a messy business and being that considerate is wonderfully loving. You might also cover the wet spot on the sheet with a soft towel so neither of you has to sleep on it.

Saturday Night # *18*

Sex and the Internet— an Introduction

T he Internet. The information superhighway. The World Wide Web. We hear about it every day, and frequently what we hear centers around how to keep children from being exposed to all the overtly sexual material that's out there. Well, you're not children, so take advantage of all the hot adult sites that are available. There's more than you could possibly look at if you surfed twenty-four hours a day forever. And it's growing every day.

Throughout this and other nights here devoted to sex on-line, I list Web sites for you to use as a jumping-off point. These sites aren't the only ones by far, and they might not even be the best. They are merely representative of what's out there at the time of this writing. If you find wonderful sites I've omitted, please write to me at joan@joanelloyd.com and let me know what you've found. I have a very active list of links and I'd love to add yours.

Have you ever logged on? If so, I don't need to tell you about the World Wide Web and everything that's available at just the tap of a few keys or the click of a mouse button. For those of you who haven't gone on-line, let me suggest that you take advantage of the free introductory offers that abound to introduce you to it. Internet service providers like America Online, Prodigy, Compuserve, as well as hundreds of smaller ones, have made access to the Net so simple with little pictures and simple instructions that anyone—and I do mean *anyone*—can log on. Just do it. You really can't destroy anything, and although it might seem daunting, it really isn't. I promise.

Once on-line, you can do anything from finding out the weather in Hong Kong to locating your best friend from high school. You can get a recipe for Hungarian goulash or instructions for planting a rosebush. You can shop for anything under the sun and visit sites you might never have imagined. And, of course, there are hundreds of adult sites, and that's where we're going to explore tonight.

Some people are afraid to surf adult sites because they fear it might become a substitute for lovemaking. The Net is only what you and your partner make of it. It's great for a warm-up, either solo, to get your juices flowing, or together, to get into the mood. In addition, together you can explore more creative ways to use your sexual energy. Ed and I surfed the Net both separately and together. Both are fun and lead to exciting evenings filled with new ideas.

There's material out there for every taste, some beautiful and some raunchy. You can read stories or buy adult toys. You can look at pictures. There are still photos, movies, and live shows of almost every type of sex act that's ever been attempted. You can join newsgroups devoted to anything you've ever thought about and receive letters from all around the world. Of course, you will also receive junk mail from all around the world.

83

I'm going to take several Saturday nights here to acquaint you with what's out there and help you to find your way around. Of course, if you'd rather just wander, begin on one Web page, find links to another page, and so on. That's fun, too, but you are going to have to wade through a lot of chaff to get to some wheat. As with everything else, whatever floats your boat.

Many of the adult sites on the Net require a membership fee, in the form of a credit card number, before you can do more than get small tastes of the material inside. A word of advice: Before you pay money for access to a site, click around and see whether you can find the material you're seeking for free. There's so much out there that there may be no reason to pay. If, after wandering, you really want to join a membership-required site, sign up for the shortest length of time possible. You can always continue your membership. Check to see whether extending your membership is automatic or whether you have to click to continue. Many of the sites I've seen have an automatic renewal policy, so if you don't tell them to stop, you'll be extended and your credit card charged without any notification. If that's what you want, just keep track of your expiration date so you can tell them not to renew well before your required date if you tire of that material.

There are many adult verification services out there, too. Through them, with one credit card number, one payment, you get access to dozens or even hundreds of sites. Do what your wallet feels is appropriate.

In the beginning of the tremendous upsurge of popularity of the Net, there was a great deal of appropriate concern about giving out credit card numbers over it. There were some quite serious security issues. Those issues have been addressed and most sites use what are called "secure servers," so that all information is properly encrypted and protected. I haven't heard recently of anyone stealing account numbers as the information whizzed by. But if you're concerned, most sites have ways to receive checks or credit card information by mail or fax.

I must take a moment here to talk about children and the Net. There are many ways for parents to attempt to keep children from viewing material they feel is unsuitable. My site, which contains adult stories and information, is protected by every service I know about so that parents can sign up for the protection service and my site will be excluded from their child's viewing. If you are interested in protecting your computer, check with http://www.cyberpatrol.com; http://www.cybersitter.com; http://www.netnanny.com; or http://www.surfwatch.com for software that blocks objectionable sites.

There are also free adult-verification schemes that purport to exclude children from objectionable material. They are based on the theory that anyone who owns a credit card must be an adult. The credit card number is supplied, verified, but no charges are recorded. Unfortunately, most of those well-intentioned attempts are doomed to failure, since the U.S. government cannot regulate non-U.S.-based sites and many of the raunchiest come from Europe and Asia.

Parents, just a word: Educate your children about sex as early as you can. Let them know your beliefs, feelings, and decisions about what's appropriate and what's not. Surf the Net and select what you feel is suitable for their age. Discuss with them why you feel other material is unsuitable, so that they integrate your morality into their own thinking. Encourage them to come to you with questions. I know it's often difficult and embarrassing to explain sexual topics to your kids, but if you don't, the Internet and their friends will. Kids are naturally curious, so the more secrets we keep, the more they will try to ferret out what they aren't supposed to know.

I have a very active Web site myself. It contains sexual advice, letters and responses from my many visitors, a new erotic story each month, and a long list of links for you to use to navigate the Net. If you want to begin your browsing here, or visit somewhere along the way, you can get there by typing http://www.joanelloyd.com. I'd love to have you visit, and drop me a line to let me know what you think.

To begin surfing, you can start with the search engines. For each, there's a box into which you type the search criteria—like "Erotic Stories" or "Naked Pictures." Once you click on "Search Now," they list anywhere from one to hundreds of sites that fit your criteria. Each search engine has a slightly different way of searching, so if you don't seem to be getting exactly what you ask for, click on their "help" or "refine search" button for additional information. Here are a few search engines to begin with:

- http://www.altavista.digital.com
- http://www.excite.com
- http://www.hotbot.com
- http://www.infoseek.com
- http://www.lycos.com
- http://www.webcrawler.com
- http://www.yahoo.com

Another way to begin surfing is to find a link site, one that has nothing but links to other sites, and then click your way from site to site. There are several particularly good link sites. Try:

- http://aosotd.com: Adult-oriented site of the day.
- http://www.adult10000.com: Webside Story. Sites here are ranked by the number of visitors they attract each day and listed in that order. The picture sites get more visitors than

the less overt ones, so they are at the top. If you're interested in nonpicture sites, head for number 500 and surf from there. This site has even got a really good search engine, so you can type in the specific kind of site you're looking for. I tried "Stories," "Bondage," and "Gay," and so forth and got lots of places to visit.

- http://www.persiankitty.com: This is a particularly good link site, since the links are divided by category, so you can find exactly what you're looking for.
- http://www.sextop1000.com/index.html: Another site that counts hits and rated sites by popularity.
- http://www.thexxxreview.com: A terrific link list to toy stores, video shops, free and pay sites, adult book stores, chat rooms, and more.

If you find a site with material that you enjoy, check out that site's links, if any. That Web master is probably directing you to other places that he or she thinks you'll enjoy. At least that's the way I do it. A word of warning, however. Many sites make money only when you pay to join, and they need visitors to make this happen. Thus, they pay other sites for advertising space, trying to encourage you to click over. Banner ads are everywhere— bright, colorful pictures with come-on advertisements splashed across the page, inviting you to click here and visit. As long as it's free and it appeals to you, have a blast.

If you find a site you particularly enjoy, make sure to "bookmark" it so you can return when you want to. Each browser has a different bookmarking procedure, so click around at the top of your screen. Eventually, you will have a permanent list of sites that intrigued you. Without bookmarks, it can be difficult to find your way back to something you particularly enjoyed.

Be warned. You'll get on a zillion mailing lists, which are

almost impossible to get off of. You'll get quite a bit of X-rated junk mail each day. I don't really mind, as I just use my delete key freely. However, I keep a separate E-mail account for Web surfing so that the so-called spam doesn't get mixed in with my real E-mail. Many Internet service providers allow you to have several identities; AOL allows up to five. With a separate password that your children won't know, you have a bit more privacy, too. You can also have a separate bookmark list for this account so that your children won't know where you've been surfing.

Here, from my links list, are a few other unusual places you might want to visit to get you started. Have fun!

- http://www.santesson.com/aphrodis/aphrhome.htm: The Aphrodisiac Home Page—a look at foods that are purported to have erotic power.
- http://www.mentertainment.com/video/101-202.htm: Batteries Not Included. This is a fun site devoted to reviews of X-rated movies.
- http://playcouples.com: The Lifestyles Organization. This comfortable and informative couples-oritented site includes chat facilities for members, an erotic art gallery, and other information and entertainment.
- http://www.masturbationpage.com: The Masturbation Home Page—facts, interviews, and good stories.
- http://www.razberry.com/raz/pink/top.htm: Pink Kink—an innovative list of "where the kink is" in romance novels (such a neat idea).
- http://www.safersex.org: The Safer Sex Organization—valuable information for all adults.
- http://www.sexuality.org: The Society for Human Sexuality—a very serious site with a tremendous amount of important information on a myriad of topics.

Okay, that's a brief introduction to the Net. For right now, let your fingers and your mouse do the walking and have fun. If you find that the Internet is as intriguing as I find it, there are several more Saturday nights here devoted to sex on the Internet. As the weeks go on, I'll introduce you to places where you can find erotic stories, pictures, places to buy toys and games, and where and how to hot-chat.

For Fun

❤️If you've bookmarked one or more erotic sites you enjoy, suggest to your partner that he or she check out your list and visit the pages. That should open new avenues of communication—after your lover gets finished making mad, passionate love to you, that is.

For Fun

❤️If you find a site that's particularly arousing, leave the computer on with that site displayed and then leave the room. Then ask your lover to get something from the computer room. The sight of the photos or situation you've left there should give him or her some great ideas.

Saturday Night # 19

A Loving Touch

Masturbation. Since our earliest years, most of us have been taught that masturbation is naughty, dirty, or even downright evil. As young girls our parents managed to dissuade us from touching our "naughty bits" and thus, through much of our lives, we have felt thoroughly intimidated. Even if nothing was said aloud, our hands were gently nudged away from our crotch and our mothers' expression was enough to give us the idea that it "wasn't nice." Women's genitals are hidden, tucked away, so that it was possible to be dissuaded. We were able to "not touch." Well, we touched when we washed but that was the only reason, and even then, we used our hands in only the most clinical way. So we never really found out how to touch ourselves and therefore couldn't teach our partners.

It's much more difficult to keep boys from learning how to touch themselves to bring pleasure. A male's pleasure zones are right out there beneath his hands, and every time he goes to the bathroom, he touches his penis. For little boys, it is only a matter of time before they learn how delightful it is to touch with a less-than-clinical hand.

As time passes, men become adept at rubbing and stroking, until the ultimate pleasure is reached, and all such comments as "You'll go blind," "You'll grow hair on your palms," or "You'll make your penis less sensitive, so you won't have any pleasure with a woman" can't deter him. I know one man who was told "You have only so many orgasms in you, so if you do that now, you won't have anything left for your wife." Amazing.

Later, in his dating career, a guy frequently asks his date, with voice or gesture, to rub his penis or, for the more brave, to take his erect penis in her mouth. He knows what he likes. Sadly for women, although her genitals are often touched to arouse her enough for intercourse, touching her genitals herself for pure enjoyment is just not done. So she remains ignorant of the pleasures of masturbation, and the details of her own body and its erogenous zones.

Tonight's game is for her only. Guys, I'm going to teach your partner how to touch herself so she can learn, and eventually teach you, what feels the best. If you want to read along, do so, and if you want to play, put some lubricant on your erect penis and show her how delicious it is for you to touch yourself. However, give her some room and some privacy. This is a very delicate business for her.

For Her

❤️ In order to learn about your personal sexuality, you first have to be comfortable with your body. How many of us are? Very few, I'm afraid. Isn't that sad? I'm fifteen pounds overweight, and since I'm almost sixty, gravity has won the ultimate victory. When

I look in the mirror, I wish it were different. So what? I'm me and I like myself, and so should you. Are you to be denied the ultimate pleasures just because we women are brought up to judge ourselves by some ridiculous standard that none of us can ever meet? No!

Let me take a few moments to fill you in on a few facts about women's bodies.

♡ There are 3 billion women who don't look like supermodels and only a few who do. And even they probably feel they have something they'd like to change.

♡ Marilyn Monroe wore a size twelve.

♡ If shop mannequins were real women, they'd be too thin to menstruate, and if Barbie were a real woman, she'd have to walk on all fours due to her proportions.

♡ The average American woman weighs 144 pounds and wears between a size twelve and a size fourteen.

♡ The models in the magazines are airbrushed—they're not perfect, either!

♡ Twenty years ago, models weighed 8 percent less than the average woman. Today, they weigh 23 percent less.

Have I made my point? Let's try to be more like men, who often pay less attention to the way they look.

Ladies, how many of you have learned how to give yourself the ultimate sexual pleasure? If you're anything like I was, you were too intimidated to try, at least for many years. I was nearly thirty before I touched myself for purely sexual reasons, and now I lament all the lost opportunities.

You must accept one thing before we begin. It's your body! There's nothing "dirty" about it. It's a beautiful thing, designed for many purposes, one of which is to receive sexual pleasure. If it weren't meant for that, women would never have sex. It's messy and awkward and we have to allow our partners to get much closer than we would under any other circumstances.

It's your body! You can touch. How can you know what's going to give you pleasure unless you've tried? How can you help your partner learn where to touch and how to touch unless you've learned and can help?

Let me tell you how I began. I had two school-aged children and a plain vanilla sex life, which was satisfying but was restricted solely to the missionary position. I'm not sure whether I had ever really climaxed. If I had, it certainly hadn't knocked my socks off. Don't get me wrong: I don't blame my ex-husband one bit. I was just as responsible for my sexual gratification as he was. We were just mutually ignorant. We had been each other's one-and-only, and *The Jerry Springer Show* hadn't been invented yet.

Oh, I read books, but they were more clinical than helpful, and the things people did in Hollywood novels were, in my mind, confined to the rich and reckless. But I was curious, and my curiosity grew as the years passed. I had always loved long, leisurely baths, so, after my children were in bed, I frequently lounged in the tub, reading a novel. One evening, whatever I read got me aroused, so I touched my inner lips. I knew they would feel slippery, and they did. I also knew that it would feel good, and it did. I will admit that back then I still had to make excuses to myself about touching my own body. It's not that I'm being bad, I told myself, I just want to learn. No overt sexual intent. I discovered my clitoris, swollen and hard, and touched it. It's hard to believe now as I write this, but I stopped. I was totally embarrassed and I quickly let the water out of the tub and dried myself off. But curiosity, once awakened, isn't buried easily. And mine wasn't.

On subsequent nights, I touched myself again, and yet again, and finally brought myself to orgasm with the handle of a toothbrush. I learned more and more, using the toothbrush and later the neck of a shampoo bottle to fill my vaginal canal while I rubbed my clitoris. I got really good at bringing myself to orgasm and found that I didn't need any stimulation other than rubbing my clitoris. I am sad to this day that I never taught my then husband what I had learned.

So, ladies, if you don't already know your body well, start now, tonight. The bathtub is a wonderful place to begin, but you can touch yourself anywhere—in bed late at night, in the shower, wherever you can be completely private, because this is, for now, a private journey. No kids, no husband, no one.

Begin by exploring with your finger. I use my middle finger, but any one will do. Touch, explore. Find the outside places that feel good. At first, unless you're aroused to begin with, your clitoris might be extrasensitive and, therefore, touching it may feel unpleasant. Do you know where it is, by the way? You'd be surprised at how many women (and men, too) don't. Just in case, it's between your outer lips, those thick fleshy ones, which are covered with pubic hair and enclose all the other parts. If you slide your fingers down your lower belly and between those lips, you'll find your clitoris, either small and almost hidden beneath a pad of flesh or sticking up, extending almost through the outer lips. It might be as small as a beebee or as large as a pencil eraser. We're all made differently.

Touch it. Go ahead and see how it feels. It might feel like a small pea, buried and difficult to find, or a swollen bean. Explore. It's okay. Really it is. Once you've found your clitoris, return to touch it from time to time as you become aroused. Slip your fingers farther back and you'll find your inner lips, thinner and more flexible, like two thick membranes that can close or open like the petals of a flower. Those lips protect the openings to the

vagina and urinary canals from clothing and dirt, and they swell and part when aroused. Slip you finger between them. If you are even a bit excited, the area between those lips will be slippery. Your body secretes a fluid, a natural lubricant to ease penile insertion. That's the way it should be.

If you're aroused but not lubricated, use some K-Y jelly or another product to lubricate the entire area. Now keep exploring. You'll find the opening to your vaginal canal. It's perfectly all right to push a finger inside and see how it feels, but take care that your hands are clean and your nails are smooth. You don't want to scratch those delicate tissues. Now, begin to make a mental list of what feels best. Do more of it. Are there things that don't feel nice? Don't do those. It's just that simple. It's your body. I can't stress that enough. You have every right to touch yourself in any way you want.

Orgasm is the eventual goal. I know that I usually emphasize that it's the journey that provides the pleasure, and that's true, but I want you to learn what pushes your body over the edge. Keep touching. Are you getting more excited? I hope so. If not, or if you want to stop for tonight, that's okay. Just do it again soon, and push yourself and your natural embarrassment further. If you don't want to stop, don't. I find that clitoral stimulation is enough to bring me to orgasm. I don't need anything inside of me, but you might be different. Or you might just want to experiment. Fingers work, although I'm not sure that most bodies are shaped properly for finger penetration. My arms just aren't long enough.

Use anything that's scrupulously clean and the right shape, long enough that it won't slip all the way in. You don't want to have to hunt for it later if it slides in too far. You can use candles, certain vegetables, purchased dildos, whatever you have that fits. Scrub the object thoroughly and be sure the surface is smooth and free from anything that might irritate. In the heat of the moment, you might not notice something scratching you.

Then just do it. Insert and withdraw or just leave the object inserted and rub your clitoris. Squeeze your vaginal muscles and feel the fullness of the penetration. If you want to touch your nipples to add another sensation, great. The more sexual stimulation, the better. Do whatever feels good. Push yourself further toward orgasm. Center your thoughts on erotic images if that helps. Tell yourself an erotic story or imagine yourself in an erotic situation. Expand on that movie scene that made your heart beat a little faster. Did a section of a romance novel curl your toes? Use that excitement to create your special fantasy. Don't judge; just flow with the feelings. Do the fingers touching you belong to Sean Penn, Jimmy Smits, Robert Redford, or even Heather Locklear? Are you being watched? Don't hesitate to use your deepest erotic feelings, and don't judge them. Use them. They belong to you, just as your body does.

I hope that as you continue to touch, you finally achieve orgasm. If you don't? Not to worry. I didn't the first time, either. It may take some time and knowledge of your body before you can climax. Continue learning. On Saturday Night #24 I'll show you how to share that knowledge with your partner in some of the most delicious ways possible.

Saturday Night #20

Saturday Night Can Begin on Monday

We've spent several months concentrating on how to make love on Saturday night. This week, let's begin our Saturday night loving on Monday morning. Here are some sexy ideas on how to tantalize, tempt, and tease your lover all week so that Saturday night will become the culmination of a week's worth of anticipation.

How can you tease your lover at work all week? Here are several ideas.

Snail Mail

This is the new name for old-fashioned letter writing. You remember. Paper. Pens. Envelopes and stamps. So write your lover a letter to be delivered at work. Include spicy details of what you two are going to do when you're together again. Mention that you spent some time at work thinking about last Saturday night and had to retreat to the bathroom to satisfy your hunger by yourself. Let your partner know you're dreaming and fantasizing about him or her.

There are card stores that specialize in erotic greetings. Send one each day to keep love sizzling. Add your own message and keep things as hot as you can.

Cassette Tapes

Lovers can keep the fires stoked by exchanging cassette tapes. That way, you can send messages of love in your own voice. Start a sexy story and then slip the tape into your partner's briefcase with a portable tape player so your partner can play it at work or while commuting. Whisper four-letter words into the microphone and combine them with some very heavy breathing.

For Her

♥♡Wrap the tape in a picture from a Victoria's Secret catalog. Tell him you've just bought that garment and can't wait to model it for him on Saturday. Or get even more explicit and wrap the tape in a pair of your panties.

For Him

♥♡Tell her how uncomfortable your slacks get every time you think of her and, if you're so inclined, also tell her what you did about it.

Telephoning

Don't overlook the fun of phone sex. To many of you, I know it sounds difficult, but it's really fun. Call your lover at work and get as down and dirty as you want and describe everything in great detail. Ask questions—like "What are you wearing?" and "How does it feel?"

For Fun

♥♡ Got two different phone lines? On Saturday afternoon, call your lover from the next room and make a few outright demands and see what happens. Yummy.

E-mail

With the phenomenal growth of the Internet, more people every day are getting E-mail accounts. It's a great way to touch your partner erotically during the long weekdays. The most wonderful thing about E-mail is that it's almost instantaneous. You usually receive a piece of mail on the same day it was sent.

With E-mail, keeping the fires fanned isn't really the problem. The difficulty is what to write.

How about beginning an erotic story, either from your own imagination or from one of the fantasies scattered through this book? You can even adapt a story from an erotica site. Then let your partner write the next chapter. Or send your lover a chapter each day. You don't have to be an expert writer, or even a good one. Remember, it's the thought that counts, not the style. You might write a story that you'd like to act out on Saturday night. Once the story's done, you two can spend time deciding what props you'll need and where you're going to act it out. You can even find an erotic photograph to E-mail. Then just add the caption: "Wouldn't this be fun?"

If your lover has only a business E-mail account, a sexy but completely circumspect note is just the thing. "Honey, I miss you. Remember that gift you got me last week? I'm thinking about it right now." You can even develop a code so that you can send "secret" messages. Maybe "I stayed in for lunch today" really means "I'm really hot for your body and can't wait for Saturday."

For Fun

❤♡There are several places on the Internet from which you can send your lover an erotic postcard. You select a sexy photograph and then add your own message. Once you send the postcard, your lover gets an E-mail message, goes to the site, and claims the card, in all its glory. Remember, many of these sites are very explicit, so be prepared. At the time of this writing, the Web pages listed below were free, but things change so quickly on the Net, this might not be the case by the time you read this.

- http://www.clpw.net/eroticcards: Here you can send pictures of women or stud-type guys on your cards. You can also add music.
- http://www.eroticcity.net/postcards/cardcenter.html
- http://www.eroticadreams.com/cards/card.html
- http://www.eroticpostcards.com
- http://www.kinkycards.com: This one's more hard-core, offering bondage photos and lots more.
• http://www.naughtycards.com

- http://www.porncards.com: There are lots of subjects for premade cards of all kinds.
- http://www.angelfire.com/tx/oscarwilly: This one also includes music to listen to while you read the card.
- http://www.southerncharms-ent.com/sce/postcards/post-card.html: Male and female cards here vary from soft and sexy to hard-core and hot.
- http://www.strip-a-gram.com: These cards are really video clips in which male and female strippers get down to boxers or G-strings, or nothing at all. They cost $3.95 but might just be worth the money.
- http://www.bobcat.net/previewb.html: There are lots of down-and-dirty images you can send.

Keeping the heat turned up to high during the week makes Saturday night all the more fun.

For Fun

❤️If you have a cell phone, call your lover from the bus or train on the way home. It's not expensive and it's really thoughtful. You might suggest that he or she meet you at the train station or bus stop for a drink and a few kisses before going home.

Saturday Night #21

Let's Go to the Movies

I have wonderful memories of my dating years. My steady date and I both lived in New York City, and when we had the money, we drove to the Bronx and went to a drive-in movie. On those evenings, we would stop at a convenient White Castle and pick up a dozen of their tiny, thin hamburgers, four orders of fries, and two large Cokes, then drive to the theater.

To see the large sign that showed which movies were playing, we had to crest a small hill. As we did, I would study the listing, and if I said, "Gee, I've been wanting to see that picture," my date would drive on to another drive-in a bit farther away. He wasn't interested in the picture at all. He was only concerned with the necking that would inevitably follow our burgers—petting that would steam the windows and rock the shock absorbers.

Let's try to re-create that feeling tonight. I know that drive-in theaters are pretty much a thing of the past, but maybe one still exists in your area. If you've got one, treasure it. It's wonderful to be alone and totally private in an atmosphere completely different from the one in which you usually play.

If you don't have a drive-in in your area, see whether there's an old theater with a balcony. Newer theaters with one level and few seats make lots of money for the owners, but what a loss to us romantics.

Okay, if you have to settle for one of the sterile ones, find the darkest spot in the back, where there's no one behind you to complain about how your kissing is blocking their view.

Next, find the right film to see. Stay away from that hit movie you've both been looking forward to and find an oldie but goodie, preferably a film with lots of romance. Avoid flicks about aliens or war unless they are so bad that you can laugh. Buy some snacks either before you arrive, if the theater allows it, or at the snack bar. Don't get chintzy. Indulge. Popcorn with lots of butter that you can lick off each other's fingers. Ice cream that's drippy and delicious and causes cold tongues that can be warmed on each other's lips.

Find your seats and cuddle close. The armrest will get in the way, of course, but do the best you can. Hold hands. Kiss. Lots of kissing with oodles of tongue and touching.

For Her

♥ Take his hand. Remember how nervous you were at the movies when you were first dating? Will he hold my hand? Will he try for a kiss? Tonight give him the go-ahead. Scratch his palm or stroke your index finger over the sensitive skin there. Suck on one of his fingers as if it were his penis. Tease. That's what this is all about.

103

For Him

♥♡While your partner is watching the movie, drape your arm around her shoulders. Remember the days when you reached around for a quick touch of breast? Go for that feeling. Don't take it for granted. Let it feel a bit sneaky. Remember that wonderful scene from *Grease* when Danny and Sandy are at the drive-in and his pretend sneeze gets his arm around her? That's the feeling you're going for tonight.

Can you actually have intercourse during the movie? I've done it at a drive-in, but it was awkward at best, even in those days when I was much more flexible and my date's car had bench seats and no gearshift lever on the floor. Tonight, however, whether you're at the drive-in or in the theater, let the excitement build. Play, rub, touch, kiss, but wait to have intercourse until you get home. It will just make the two of you hotter, and that's the whole idea.

For Fun

♥♡Dress for the movie in clothing that makes it easy for your partner to play.

For Her

♥♡How about a sweater with a deep neckline or one that buttons or zips up the front? If you're feeling particularly bold, wear a skirt, maybe with no undies.

For Him

❤♡Consider not wearing any shorts beneath your jeans. Not only will it be easy for her to delve into the hidden regions, but the feeling of your naked genitals rubbing against the inside of your zipper will be tremendously arousing.

Saturday Night #22

Got Some Money to Spend?

If you've got a few dollars to spend on a dream date for this Saturday night, here are some ideas for an exotic evening.

- ♡ Rent a limo and make love in the backseat.
- ♡ Dine at an expensive restaurant—and no underwear allowed.
- ♡ Buy a fancy basket and fill it with massage oil, bubble bath, a few condoms, and maybe a new bedroom toy.
- ♡ Buy your partner something scandalous—skimpy and silk or exotic and leather—and wrap it with a story or tape inside, detailing the activities to come.
- ♡ Rent a convertible and drive on the highway with the top down.
- ♡ Buy several bouquets of flowers, spread them around the bedroom, and make love "in the garden."

♡ Plan an evening at one of those hedonistic resorts—you know, the ones with the vibrating beds and the heart-shaped hot tubs. Many of them are garish, but it's fun for an evening. Make all the plans, but don't tell your lover any details until you arrive.

♡ Buy a Polaroid camera and wrap it up as a gift. Include a nude photo of yourself and a gift certificate for more photos to come.

♡ Buy a bottle of champagne, take it home, and drink it from your cupped palms. For fun, make mimosas, two parts champagne to one part orange juice, and serve in fancy glasses. For more of a kick, add a shot of orange brandy, like Triple Sec or Cointreau.

♡ Have an outrageous meal catered by your favorite restaurant. Many non-take-out places will cater if you ask and include a big tip. Then set up a table in the bedroom and indulge.

♡ Get a large furry throw and put it over the passenger seat of the car. Ask your partner to take off his or her underpants and sit on the fur with a bare bottom. This feels sexy for men as well as for women.

♡ Send a limo to pick your lover up from work. Be sure to include a bottle of champagne and some soft music.

♡ Take a trip to a sex shop with a designated amount of money that the two of you "have to spend." That forestalls the "I don't know what to buy," or "Everything's so expensive." If you haven't got a sex shop in your area, catalogs or the Internet will do. (Other Saturday nights here will explore these two delicious ways to shop.)

♡ Buy several new CDs by his or her favorite singer and fill the bedroom with sweet sounds.

♡ Buy a set of satin sheets. Be a bit careful when you make

love on them, however. I've found it's really hard to get a grip with your fingers or toes. This can lead to giggles and ultimately great lovemaking. If satin isn't your thing, new flannel sheets in the winter can be deliciously soft and cuddly.

♡ A large piece of leather spread on the bed can change your lover's whole attitude. The smell, the feel, and the idea of leather all combine to create a hedonistic atmosphere. It's worth a try.

♡ Buy her some skimpy panties or get him some satin shorts; then cut a hole in the middle of the front to provide easy access for your hand during the evening.

♡ Spend an evening at an amusement park and fool around at the top of the Ferris wheel. Take several rides, until you're both so hot and bothered that home seems too far away. Is there a convenient motel?

Saturday Night #23

Got No Money in Your Jeans?

*H*ere are some ideas for things you can do tonight on a tight (or nonexistent) budget.

Plan for the evening by getting rid of the kids. If you've got uncles, aunts, or grandparents, impose a bit on them for an evening. No relatives? Send the little darlings off to a neighbor's house, with the understanding that you'll reciprocate sometime soon. Then think of something particularly delicious to do with your suddenly free time.

♡ Set a timer and slow-dance naked. Maybe make a deal that there will be no touching with hands until the record stops.

♡ Make your lover a midnight snack and serve it in bed. Use a linen napkin and shining silverware if you have them and, if possible, put a flower on the tray. Then serve it naked. Remember, you're the dessert.

♡ Here's something I find really erotic. Take a belt, a length of fabric, or part of an old shirt in as wide a width as you can find and fasten it very tightly around your partner's waist. The feeling of being encased is really stimulating, and when worn beneath clothing, it leads to a day of anticipation.

♡ Gift certificates are a wonderful way to give a present without spending any money. Erotic gift certificates? How about a year's supply of erotic massages or one that just says, "I'll do *anything* you like for an entire evening."

♡ If you have access to the Internet, go to http://www.virtualflowers.com and send her a free virtual bouquet. Sign the card with a silly message like "Happy Arbor Day" or "Happy Millard Fillmore's Birthday."

♡ Combine five hundred dollars of play money and a catalog and insist that your partner "spend" every cent. Then do some creative thinking. It's amazing what an ingenious mind can come up with for very little money.

♡ Dig out the Christmas lights and use them to light the bedroom.

♡ Create a greeting card using a computer program, if you have one, or just scissors and paper. Inside, detail what you have in mind for the evening's activities. Slip the card in his or her lunch.

♡ Create an imaginary love potion from some herb tea and flavorings. Show it to your partner and then drink it. From then on, you're a love slave, committed to doing anything your "owner" wishes. Or ask your lover to drink it and become yours.

♡ Play a game of strip gin rummy. And wear lots of clothes so that it takes awhile to undress before it "gets good."

♡ This sounds like such a small thing, but it really says a lot. With your partner watching you, unplug the TV. Commit yourselves to an evening together, loving and being loved in all ways, shapes, and forms.

♡ Tune the clock radio to an easy-listening station and set it for 3:00 A.M. When it goes off, cuddle, snuggle, and stroke. Then do what comes naturally.

♡ Play the following game. "How long can I tease you without you reaching orgasm?" See whether you can drive your lover over the edge despite his or her best intentions. The effort not to come can make sex all the more erotic. One version of this casts her in the roll of a lap dancer. She can do anything, including pressing her breasts against his face, but he cannot use his hands. Or he can rub his erect penis over her face, but she cannot lick or touch.

♡ Make a "Sex Partner Wanted" ad and include all the things you'd really like your partner to do. Include a few secrets if you want. Then let your lover pick one thing to specialize in for that evening. Maybe your partner will make up something like it for you, so you'll know what he or she really wants.

Saturday Night #24

Sharing Your Loving Touch

*T*onight, you're going to do something you probably thought you'd never do. You're going to show your partner how you pleasure yourself. If you've spent any time masturbating, you know better than anyone exactly what gives you the most pleasure. So now it's time to show your partner, to teach him or her while you pleasure yourself.

It's really difficult to touch yourself during lovemaking. For me, it took a lot of repetitions of "Show me how you please yourself" for me to believe that it was all right to touch myself while Ed watched. He'll think he doesn't satisfy me, I thought. Actually, nothing could have been further from the truth. I discovered that he gets immense pleasure from watching my fingers while I touch myself, even while we're having intercourse. He loves to see me give myself pleasure. Now, I get a manicure every week so I have long, bright, shiny nails.

He says it's really sexy, and I love the way his eyes light up when I touch myself. And he's learned what I like by watching.

The same goes for a woman watching a man. We weren't born knowing how to "give a hand job." How can we learn unless you men teach us? Show us what you like. Do you like short, fast strokes or long, slow ones? Do you like to use one hand or two? Don't keep us guessing when it just takes a bit of bravery to give us a live demonstration.

Here's how to start. Let's say you're both really excited. You're touching your partner, learning what gives the most pleasure. You've done a little hot talking, with your warm breath against your lover's ear. There's lots of kissing. Now whisper, "I want to see how you pleasure yourself. Please show me." Take your lover's hand and place it on his or her genitals. "Show me, baby." Then move your hand away. And please, don't stop kissing and being supportive. This is really difficult. "It will make me so hot to watch you. Please." Stop touching your partner now, so there will be no choice if he or she wants more pleasure. Let your lover's satisfaction depend on his or her hands. "So sexy. So hot. I want to see."

If you sense your partner's really reluctant for you to watch, start with the lights out and just your hand over his or hers. "Show me." You can't see, of course, but you can feel. "It's so erotic. Please." Encourage but don't force. Tease and tempt. Many find the word *masturbate* an erotic turn-on. Try saying, "Masturbate for me." It might just be the spark that ignites wonderful things. Make a deal if you need to. "You show me, and then I'll show you how I do it."

If this idea doesn't work the first time, take time another night. It might take several Saturdays before you two are able to demonstrate masturbation for the first time, and even longer before you can really show your partner how you like to be touched. It's well worth the effort, and remember, some Saturday nights take a bit of effort.

113

Saturday Night #*25*.

Erotic Beginnings
—Part 2

*E*arlier in the book, I wrote the beginnings of a number of fantasies for you to play with. I hope you found one that got your juices flowing. Here are some more for you to read and then complete. For tonight, I've written about unseen strangers twice, one from a woman's point of view and one from a man's. Of course, there's always playing doctor, too. Enjoy!

HER UNSEEN STRANGER

The business dinner party was very formal, held at an exclusive country club, and Elaine had been dreading it for weeks. Glasses of champagne and tiny hors d'oeuvres were passed around by silent, formally dressed servers but even after two glasses of bubbly, her slight buzz did nothing to relax her. As the treasurer of the company, her attendance had been mandatory, and she had spent most of the early evening talking finance with several of the firm's clients. Now she stood to one side, really bored, wondering whether she could stop smiling, even for a moment.

As she stood, she caught the eye of a man she'd never seen before and begun a subtle eyeball flirt, glancing at him, holding his gaze, then watching him look away first. It wasn't anything serious, but it helped her pass the time. She imagined him sweeping her off her feet and whisking her away from the group.

"Ladies and gentlemen," her boss said, interrupting her fantasy, "dinner is served."

She smoothed the skirt of her teal-blue knee-length dress and made her way into the dining room. She found her assigned seat between two very important clients and began to give them the subtle sales pitch that was expected of her.

Dinner passed slowly, with several courses of rich, complicated food. Finally, as dessert and coffee were served, the lights in the room dimmed and her boss moved to a platform. In the spotlight, he began his speech.

Elaine listened in the near-darkness, sipping her coffee and trying not to yawn. Suddenly, she felt hands on her ankles, fingers sliding up the inside of her legs, pushing her skirt upward and her knees apart. She couldn't believe what was happening, but there they were, those hands.

She knew she should scream, or stand up and move back, but she didn't want to make a scene. She tried to slide her chair backward, but it wouldn't move. The hands were very talented, stroking and tickling, arousing her. She pulled at the long tablecloth, anxious to see what was going on beneath the table, but the cloth was very full and the room too dark to see anything.

Lips replaced the fingers and she knew she didn't want to

move. She wouldn't move. She stared in the direction of the speaker and tried to keep her eyes open as the hands and mouth aroused her. She couldn't do this. But she let the mouth do whatever it wanted. She couldn't do anything else.

His Unseen Stranger

It was just five o'clock and Dave had a dinner meeting to attend. He was really late. He had a cab waiting, but for now he stood, waiting for the elevator to whisk him from his office on the twentieth floor. He glanced at his watch and tapped his foot. The ding and lighted arrow indicated that the leftmost elevator had arrived at his floor and was going down. He grabbed his briefcase in one hand and, juggling a large notebook in the other, marched to the elevator and stepped inside. Everyone moved slightly to accommodate his filled arms. He paid little attention to the other occupants, ten or eleven people all heading for the lobby.

At the eighteenth floor, the elevator stopped and two women added their bodies to the crush already inside. Dave wiggled a bit, making room for himself, trying not to touch any of the other people in the car.

Two more stops added three more occupants and people were now unable to keep from pressing against one another. Suddenly, between seven and six, the elevator lurched to a stop and the lights went out. There wasn't even an emergency light. In the pitch-black, someone said, "It's stopped."

Brilliant, he thought. Now I'm going to be even later. He saw a dim light as someone activated a cell phone. "No service," a voice muttered.

"Push the emergency button," someone said, and immediately the din of the bell filled the car.

The phone on the emergency panel rang. Dave heard someone open the panel, pick up the receiver, and say, "Yes? Really? Okay." Dave could hear the phone replaced in its cradle.

"It looks like we're stuck here for a little while. There's a blackout. This block and maybe more. We're not getting out of here anytime soon, I guess."

"Oh shit."

"Oh, no!"

"It's really dark. Aren't there any emergency lights?"

"No, I guess it's going to stay dark."

Dave set his briefcase down and hugged his notebook. Suddenly, he felt someone grab his behind. Questing fingers squeezed his buttocks. He tried to wiggle away, but he was trapped in the press of bodies in the darkened elevator. A soft voice whispered in his ear. "Don't say anything. Just feel." Lips pressed against the back of his neck and a soft tongue licked a trail from his hairline to his shirt collar.

He knew he should say something, yet he didn't. Teeth nibbled at the side of his neck and the hands roamed his back. What was he going to do?

He closed his eyes, let his head fall back, and did nothing. As the voice had said, he just felt as the hands slipped around his waist.

PLAYING DOCTOR

Steve had been planning it for several days. He'd gotten ahold of a set of scrubs like the ones doctors wear and a pair of latex gloves. He'd even asked a friend who worked in a doctor's office to get him one of those paper gowns that people wear for exams. A few cotton balls soaked with alcohol lay in a dish beside the bed to add the right smell to the room, and he'd moved the

117

goosenecked lamp from the den to the bedside table and spread a white sheet over the bed. Now all he needed was for Debbie to get home from the office.

"Honey, I'm home," her voice cried out.

"I'm here," he yelled, turning on the bright light and extinguishing all the other lights in the room. "You're just in time for your appointment."

The door opened. "What appointment?" Debbie said, striding into the bedroom.

"The doctor's waiting. I was afraid I'd have to take the next patient." Steve could see the wheels turning in his wife's brain and he watched the gleam suddenly appear in her eyes.

"Oh, y-y-yes," she stammered. "I almost forgot."

Steve handed his wife the paper gown and pointed toward the bathroom. "Why don't you change while I get ready here?" While Debbie watched, he pulled on the pair of gloves, snapping the rubbery cuffs loudly. She watched and a blush washed over her face.

"Of course," she said, her voice breathy. "Yes."

As she walked into the bathroom, Steve smiled.

If you want to jump ahead to the third set of erotic beginnings, skip to Saturday Night #34.

Saturday Night #26

Light Reading and Heavy Breathing

Reading an erotic story is a particularly delicious way to get your libido into gear, and that's what we're going to do tonight. In a story, sex is perfect. No one ever makes a wrong move or gets a cramp in her foot. Life isn't like that, of course, and maybe that's why we like to read about perfect sex. Do you enjoy a good hot story? I know I do. I used to delude myself that I just enjoyed the erotic scenes in books because they advanced the story. Yeah, right. The hot scenes were fun to read because they made me hot, and still do.

If you want to read erotic stories, there are hundreds of books devoted to erotic short stories. Try my book *Bedtime Stories for Lovers,* for example, or one of my erotic novels, like *Velvet Whispers* (okay, okay, small commercial).

Many large chain bookstores have sections devoted to erotica, and others have erotic fiction mixed in with the self-help books on relationships and sexuality. Two books I particularly enjoyed are *Erotic Interludes* by Lonnie Barbach and *Forbidden Flowers* by Nancy Friday. You might also check the fiction section for collections of shorter erotic tales. I can suggest the *Best American Erotica* short story collections, edited by Susie Bright, and the *Herotica* collections, edited by Susie Bright or Marcy Sheiner. Taste in erotic literature is very personal, however, so you might need to browse to find what really gets your juices flowing.

There are dozens of magazines devoted to sexy stories. Several are in letter format, like *Penthouse Forum* and my particular favorite, *Variations*. Other magazines combine pictures with fiction, many devoted to areas of special interest, like coeds or women with large breasts. Big-city newsstands have a tremendous selection. In smaller towns, it might be difficult to find such magazines, but the search is well worth the effort.

Buying explicit books and magazines isn't as difficult as you might think, either. The checkout clerk really doesn't care what you're reading. He or she just zaps the bar code over the scanner and takes your money. You really aren't judged by your choices. Honest.

Before the advent of the Internet, finding stories to read used to be more difficult than it now is. Whether you read stories to share, to communicate, or just to heat you up a bit, the Internet is full of them.

How to find stories on the Net? First, be sure that your Web browser/Internet service provider doesn't have parental controls, or if it does, that it is set to allow you full access to the Web. I'm on AOL and they have very strict controls, which you can alter to suit your needs. Hunt around the options on your system and fix them as you choose. And if your children use the same account you do, be sure that you return the control settings to the childproof ones when you're finished browsing.

On a previous Saturday night, I suggested several places to

begin to surf the Net, and I list more at the end of this Saturday night. And be assured, there's something for every taste, and more. But besides surfing, if you want to read erotic stories, you might want to join a newsgroup; they exist by the hundreds. A newsgroup is an Internet system whereby letters, stories, and advertisements on a particular subject are sent to a central address and then are posted for all the members of the group to read. Some groups have only one or two postings per day; others have dozens. You can receive the mail and never send, or you can respond to any letter that intrigues you.

Newsgroups exist for almost any topic imaginable, from fly-fishing to restoring your '57 Chevy. On AOL, any newsgroup can be subscribed to quite easily. Each Internet service provider, or ISP, and each browser has its own way for you to join a newsgroup, so you might need to click around to discover the way yours handles it. With some, the postings come right to your mailbox, while on others, you have to go to a particular site to read your newsgroup's most recent additions.

There are two types of newsgroups, moderated and non-moderated. If the group is moderated, then someone reads every submission before it's posted. This prevents the myriad advertisements and pieces of junk mail from becoming part of your daily flood. On the other hand, it also prevents things that you might want, like ads for new story sites. So choose a newsgroup and see what happens. If it's not to your taste, either in content or number of postings, cancel the subscription and select one or more new ones.

There are myriad groups devoted to sexual topics, several specializing in erotic stories. Some have wonderful stories, and some are just plain awful. Most are in between, and every one of us has different tastes anyway.

Since most of these aren't moderated, a lot of your newsgroup mail will be advertisements for everything from Web sites to professional entertainers inviting you to call and chat—for a fee. But a few good stories can be worth the effort. In addition, if you've ever wanted to try your hand at an erotic tale, it's a great way to see your story in print and to get some feedback. If you post a story, you can ask readers to drop you a note and let you know whether they liked it.

To find newsgroups that might appeal to your particular tastes, many Internet service providers have their own searching mechanisms, and they are necessary, since there are so many newsgroups out there. If you want, you can try http://www.dejanews.com, a newsgroup search engine into which you can enter any topic and find groups and specific postings that fit your needs. I searched just now on "Erotic Stories" and found more than thirty references.

Here are a few specific newsgroups to begin with:

- alt.sex
- alt.sex.stories.moderated
- alt.sex.bondage
- alt.stories.erotic
- rec.arts.erotica

Many amateur and professional writers enjoy sharing their tales with visitors. Many are free. The Web is growing and changing faster than can be controlled, however, and it's difficult to keep track of the changes. The sites here contained lots of free stories as of the time of this writing.

- http://www.joanelloyd.com: I have to begin with my own site, of course. I post an original story of mine each month and there are excerpts from my books, as well. And my links list is filled with other erotic story sites, like those below.
- http://www.adultstorycorner.com: Lots of good stories, tastefully presented.

- http://annejet.pair.com: Anne's Erotic Stories Archive.
- http://www.xstories.com: Stories by Angela Preston.
- http://www.connectx.com/cyntil8ing: A fine collection of stories.
- http://www.pair.com/~julie: Erotica by Julie.
- http://users.lanminds.com/~mohanraj/home.html: Mary Anne's wonderful stories.
- http://www.nifty.org: A tremendous, well-organized collection of stories, many gathered from postings to newsgroups.
- http://www.cadvision.com/jove: Satin Sheets—Erotica by Jove.

There are hundreds more. Use these as a jumping-off point and then browse to your heart's content.

For Fun

♥♡Cut a story out of a magazine or print one from a Web site. Then put the tale under your lover's pillow or slip it into his or her briefcase for some *quiet reading*.

For Fun

♥♡Have you ever considered writing your own erotic short story? It's not as difficult as you might think. Reach into your own personal collection of fantasies and write one down, in outrageous detail. It doesn't have to be good or grammatically correct, since it's just for your own enjoyment or for sharing with your partner. You can even write just the *setup,* the part of the story in which he or she begins to play, or use one from the Erotic Beginnings sections in this book as a starting point. Then you and your partner can alternate chapters. How hot will it get? The sky's the limit.

123

We've Reached the Halfway Point

O kay, we've played for twenty-six weeks so far, and I know that your sex life is better than it was six months ago. Maybe you've ventured into totally new areas of enjoyment, or just picked up a few bits and pieces along the way.

Well, there's still quite a way to go. There are still fantasies lurking in the back of your mind, things that you've never risked telling your partner about. Want to watch an erotic movie, or make one yourself? Want to play with grown-up toys? Want to hot-chat over the Internet or shave your genitals?

In the next half a year, you'll get your chance, so let's go!

Saturday Night #27

Rubbing It In

$\mathcal{E}$rotic massage. Ever wanted to give one? Tonight, give it a try. Before you go any further, however, make sure that both of you agree on the type of massage you're going to give. Although it's wonderful to have a back rub when you're tense or a leg massage when you've been on your feet all day, tonight's body rub is for arousal. It isn't going to be therapeutic, although in the beginning, it may be difficult to tell the difference. This one's going to end up with good hot sex, so be sure both of you know and agree to that beforehand. It can be a drag for one person to expect relaxation and the other to anticipate excitement.

Let's start with a location: The bed's usually the most convenient place. There are, of course, narrow massage tables that allow the masseur or masseuse to be at the correct height and to get around to all sides, but few of us have one, so the bed's just going to have to do. Cover the surface with a large piece of plastic to protect the sheets. An old plastic tablecloth or a painting drop cloth will do, and any variety store will have something that will work. Cover the plastic with a thick layer of towels or blankets. Here's a tip—put a few towels in the dryer and spread them on the bed just before your lover arrives. That yummy warmth adds to the sensation. And put one towel or blanket aside to cover the parts of your partner that you're not touching right now. It keeps your partner warm and makes it feel a bit safer. Oh, yes, unplug the phone. No distractions allowed.

Put on some soft music if you like, or just enjoy the silence. Light candles, turn the lights down low or cover a lamp with a scarf, taking care to keep any fabric far from the heat of the lightbulb. Burn some incense or use an aromatherapy burner to give the air a sexy scent. And turn up the heat in the bedroom so it's nice and toasty. That way, both of you can eventually get naked together. Open a bottle of wine and pour two glasses. Both of you can sip as the evening progresses.

You'll need something to make your hands and your partner's body slippery. In my experience, most body lotions disappear into the skin too quickly, so if you're going to use that, use lots and reuse often. There are lots of packaged preparations, but it's not necessary to use expensive massage oil; cooking oil will do. You can use a smooth vegetable oil, like sweet almond oil, sleek and wonderful to the skin, but even corn, sunflower, grapeseed, or safflower oil will do. Stay away from olive, palm, and coconut oils, all of which are too thick and will thicken even more as you work. Try to use an oil that's not scented. You want to think sex, not salad. And if you want to get really fancy, try avocado or jojoba oil.

Consider adding a few drops of an essential oil. This isn't the kind of food flavoring you find in the supermarket, but, rather, *127* the type of oil you'll probably find at your neighborhood health-food store (or see the list on page 129.) Try a combination of ylang-ylang and black pepper or juniper and sandalwood. Although essential oils seem very expensive (about twenty dollars for a small bottle in my local health-food store, less if you buy from a specialty source found through the Internet), you use only a few drops. Experiment with quantities. Start small, with about five teaspoons of base oil with two or three drops of essential oil or oils. Remember, you can always add, but you can't remove drops once in the mix.

A friend who's a licensed massage therapist recommends that once you find a mix you enjoy, make up a larger quantity so you can give a massage on the spur of the moment. She begins with an eight-ounce plastic container with a squeeze or flip top. If you use a bottle with a top that screws on, you'll have a difficult time later unscrewing the lid with oily hands. Then add some vitamin E. It's nice for the skin and acts as a preservative. Keep the container in the refrigerator between uses and it will keep almost indefinitely. But if you open the bottle and the contents don't smell nice, the oil might have become rancid. Throw it out and begin again.

Always test a bit of the oil on both yourself and your partner to be sure there's no possibility of painful skin reactions. Stroke some on the inside of your wrist and some on your partner's the day before you want to use it and see what happens. Don't wash the area for twenty-four hours. If either of you develop any redness, itching, swelling or the like, don't use that oil. Try something else.

If you're interested in aromatherapy, the use of essential oils for healing and mood alteration, here are a few books you might enjoy. They all have recipes for specific combinations of oils for erotic enhancement.

- *Aromatherapy Blends and Remedies* by Franzesca Watson and Christine Lane (Thorsons Publishers, 1996)
- *The Art of Sensual Aromatherapy* by Nitya Lacroix, with Sakina Bowhay (Henry Holt, 1995)
- *The Complete Book of Essential Oils and Aromatherapy* by Valerie Ann Worwood (World Library, 1991)
- *500 Formulas for Aromatherapy: Mixing Essential Oils for Everyday Use* by David Schiller and Carol Schiller (Sterling Publications, 1994)

If you've got access to the Internet, there are lots of sites devoted to aromatherapy information and sales. You can purchase oils more inexpensively than in the local health-food store. Use any search engine you like. I went to http://www.altavista.digital.com, then clicked on their "Health and Fitness" category, and on "Alternative Medicine," "More Therapies A–Z," and "Aromatherapy." I found several dozen sites listed there.

For information about aromatherapy oils try:
- http://www.fragrant.demon.co.uk: A guide to aromatherapy.
- http://www.aromaweb.com: Aroma Web.
- http://www.zuzuspetals.net: Tips, a catalog, and a bulletin board.

To purchase oils try:
- http://www.crystalmountain.com: Crystal Mountain Oils and Incenses.
- http://www.evb-aromatherapy.com: Elizabeth Van Buren Aroma Therapy.
- http://moonrise.botanical.com/aroma/aroma.html: Moonrise Herbs.
- http://www.poyanaturals.com: Poya Essential Oils.

129

Here's a warning: If you're going to get anything near a woman's delicate tissues or a man's anus, never use any petroleum product for massage—for example, baby or mineral oil. They are difficult to remove, particularly from internal vaginal areas, and provide a great host for all kinds of bacteria. Petroleum products also break down the latex in gloves or condoms, causing microscopic holes that allow microorganisms to pass through.

Now that you've mixed the oil, heat it to just above body temperature in the microwave or keep the bottle in a container of warm water. Take care. Your hands are much less sensitive to heat than her back or his chest, so be sure of the temperature before using. Test a bit on the inside of your forearm. If it's too warm, wait a few minutes or add a bit more cold oil. And if it's a bit too cool, rub your hands together for a moment before touching your lover.

Have your partner lie down on his or her stomach and get comfortable. You might add a folded towel beneath the forehead and ankles and, for a woman, beneath the hips. Later, when he or she turns over, the towel can be repositioned beneath the knees or neck. Cover your partner's legs and buttocks with a towel or blanket until you want to touch there.

Place your hands gently on your partner's back and just relax together as you give soft, gentle, soothing strokes. Try to keep your hands in contact with your partner's body at all times, proceeding from long strokes to deeper ones. If you need to add more oil, lean the back of your hand against your partner, and pour more oil into the cup of your palm without ever losing contact with his or her skin. A word of warning before you begin. If your partner has any sort of injury, don't massage that area without first consulting your lover's doctor.

Okay, now what? Where do I touch? How? You touch anywhere you want to. Cover most of your partner's well-massaged back to keep in the warmth and move on to someplace easy, like feet or hands. Have you ever had a hand massage? Just delicious.

Go slowly and repeat your strokes several times to allow him or her to revel in the sensations. Pay careful attention to your partner's reactions. See what makes his or her hips move, what elicits a groan or a sigh. If something seems to make your partner uncomfortable, go somewhere else. The most difficult part of beginning erotic massage is to be able to gauge the excitement level of your partner. Before you begin, suggest that he or she help by making desires as evident as possible, up to and including asking for what's wanted.

Don't overlook the face. Soft touching and strokes over the lips, cheeks, and forehead feel wonderful. Unless your partner objects, run your fingers through his or her hair and rub the scalp, an amazingly sensitive area.

Tease. Take a while before approaching a sensitive area. Play. Stroke toward the nipples or groin without touching. Make your partner really want it . . . badly. And, if you think he or she will enjoy it, pinch a bit when things get hot. Make yourself felt, moving toward a sexy ending.

When you've reached the erotic section, try covering your naked chest with oil and stretching out, full length, over your partner and using your entire body to rub your partner's. If you want to know specifically how to touch your partner's genitals, skip to Saturday Night #33.

Let nature take its course. Do what feels good at a particular moment. Keep sipping your wine and try to lose those inhibitions. Aren't there places you've always wanted to touch? Go for it. You'll never find a better time.

There are lots of good books on the subject of massage, both therapeutic and erotic. If you want to get serious, pick up one or more from your local library or a bookstore. Try:

- *The New Sensual Massage* by Gordon Inkeles and Karla K. Austin (Arcata Arts, 2nd edition, 1998)
- *Erotic Massage: The Tantric Art of Love* by Kenneth Ray Stubbs and Louise-Andree Saulnier (J.P. Tarcher, 1999)
- *Anne Hooper's Ultimate Sexual Touch: The Lovers' Guide to Sensual Massage* by Anne Hooper (DK Publishing, 1995)

It's often suggested that one partner massage the other, then switch places. That's all well and good, but I think that getting up and massaging your partner right after a good relaxing massage or a rousing sexual encounter ruins the mood. It might be better to delay the second massage until another evening. And a massage gift certificate makes a terrific present, maybe wrapped around a starter kit of exotic oils.

A final word: Don't take it all too seriously. If you want to giggle, do so. If you want to stop in the middle and make love, great. As with everything else that's new, take your time, experiment, and have fun.

Saturday Night #28

Make a Winter Night Sizzle

Baby, it's cold outside, but it can be warm and sexy inside. Here are some warmer-uppers for a cold Saturday night.

♡ Try a winter-evening heater. Brew some really good coffee and pour a cup for both you and your lover. Then heat it up with some Bailey's Irish Cream or a bit of Cointreau, Frangelico, Kahlúa, or any other liqueur or whiskey you've got around.

♡ Bring some snow inside and play during lovemaking. The cold on the skin at just the right moment can be explosive.

♡ Open all the windows, pull the quilt up to your noses, and huddle together for warmth.

♡ Tuck a piece of silk or fur inside your bra or shorts during the day as you prepare for Saturday evening. It will sensitize your skin for your partner's touch.

♡ Find some suntan lotion and rub it on your face. That coconut scent will make you both feel like summer vacations and good hot sex.

♡ Make love in the car with windows open. And if you've got a sunroof, better still. Cold? Keep each other warm.

♡ Spread a fluffy blanket in front of the fireplace and get naked on it. With a roaring fire, it's even nicer. Obvious? Yes, but we're often too busy even to bother with the obvious.

♡ Pretend it's too cold to get undressed, so make love with your clothes on.

♡ Put on your winter coat with nothing beneath. Let the furry or silky lining caress your skin.

♡ Got access to a hot tub? Turn the bubbles up and fool around beneath the water.

♡ Recently, Ed and I bought some mulling spices especially designed for use with red wine. You heat wine, then drop in the bag of spices and let simmer. Wonderful for a cold night.

♡ Share a hot shower. If you've got one, play with a handheld massager and spray all the delicious parts. And when you shower, use a bit of your hair conditioner on your pubic hair. It will make it softer and change your scent.

♡ In the shower, rub each other all over with one of those scrubbies that come with body wash. They're just a bit rough and make the skin tingle all over.

And here are a few more fun things to try, hot or cold.

♡ In a group at a restaurant or at a party? Lean very close and whisper sexy things in your lover's ear. Both the subject matter and the heat of your breath make this a really erotic pleasure. When you're done, a quick tongue lick can seal a bargain.

♡ Here's a silly one that can lead anywhere you want. Undress each other—without using your hands.

♡ Rent an outrageous X-rated film and watch it in bed together. If you see something you want to try, stop the film and say, "Let's do *that. Now!*"

Saturday Night #29

One Picture

Pictures. Centerfold. Skin flicks. Dirty movies. Stag films. There are more still and moving pictures available now than ever, and they are more popular. Tonight, let's explore the pleasures of looking at erotic images, either alone or with your lover.

Erotic pictures probably began right around the time that the first caveman drew a picture of an antelope on the wall of a cave. Somewhere, there was probably also a drawing of a naked cavewoman. Why? Because men liked to look at them then, and they still do today. And don't sell women short in the picture department, either. Remember Burt Reynolds wearing nothing but a staple in his navel?

Cave paintings gave way to the great masters, who gloried in the naked human form and painted well-endowed men, voluptuous women, and various mythological beasts doing just about everything it was possible to do. Great art? Of course. The dirty pictures of their time? You bet. I wonder whether those old masters would have gotten quite as many commissions if all their men and women had been clothed. We'll never know, of course. Oh, and don't forget great statues. Think about Michelangelo's *David* in almost all of his glory. Hmm. A well-developed guy if I ever saw one.

So folks have been looking at "dirty" pictures since the world began. Now it's gotten incredibly easy. On just about every newsstand, you'll find *Playboy* and *Penthouse* and dozens of other slick magazines devoted to the glorification of the female and male form. No more sneaking a peek at French postcards. You can get more than ever in each issue. Blondes, brunettes, and redheads with large breasts and flat stomachs, guys with well-developed pecs and, even better, thighs. It doesn't have to be overt. Have you noticed the cover of *Cosmopolitan*? Take a good look at the *Baywatch* men and women, Xena: Warrior Princess, Seven of Nine on *Star Trek: Voyager,* or Hercules, if you haven't already. Not quite centerfolds, but close enough.

Why do folks look at erotic pictures? Because they excite. Do we regular humans suffer by comparison? Probably. Those magazine photos are carefully posed and then airbrushed. The models, male and female, are the cream of the crop, and gorgeous in a way that most of us never were and never will be. And? Should we be jealous? Forbid our mates from ever looking? Even if we did, it wouldn't work. I remember the expression on my date's face when I quite obviously ogled a well-built guy in a tight shirt and a pair of brief running shorts who ran by the window of the restaurant in which we were dining. "You mean women look at men?" he asked, truly incredulous, as my head swiveled to stare at a gorgeous pair of buns. I filled him in on my philosophy. Anyone who says they don't look at an attractive body is blind, dead, or lying. But we don't touch.

People look, and that's that. Even if your partner likes to look at pictures of naked models, remember that it's you that he or she will be with tonight. So get into the spirit.

137

The common wisdom is that women aren't as turned on by visual images as men are. Actually, I'm not aroused by still photos, but I'm turned on by a good (and there aren't many) erotic film more than Ed is. Neither of us find centerfolds of either sex a turn-on, but many find the perfection of the centerfold exciting. "Different strokes for different folks." So relax. You might find you enjoy looking, too. Even if you don't particularly enjoy it, you can relish the way your partner gets turned on—and then makes passionate love to you.

Where to find erotic pictures? You all know about the magazines that exist. They are numerous and usually shrink-wrapped, and can be found on the upper shelves of the magazine racks.

For Her

♥♡ This week, actually look at one of the magazines that you haven't dared look at before. You know the ones, those that have pictures of sexy, half-naked (or all-naked) guys, like *Playgirl.* Try to open your mind and see what all the fuss is about. And while you're looking, let loose of some of your inhibitions. Open up to the erotic possibilities of titillating images. Now, dare yourself to buy one! Go ahead, do it. And when you get home, open it and look. It's okay, really.

Personally, I find a love scene in a good R-rated movie much more provocative than something more overt, but I've enjoyed a few X-rated films in my time, too. If you're interested, try renting one. Marilyn Chambers has starred in a few I've liked, *Insatiable* and *Up and Coming,* and you might try the films produced by Femme Productions, like *Three Daughters* or *Urban Heat.* Candida Royalle, the founder of Femme Productions, has a Web site, by the way—at http://www.royalle.com—where you can read short bits about her films and purchase them if you like.

You can also try the films with titles that are knockoffs of recent films, or the ones with specialties like women of color, lesbian relations, men with twelve-inch erections, or even a film featuring a man with two penises. Well, you get the idea. Some of the large chain video-rental stores don't carry X-rated films, but I'm sure you'll find a store in your area that does.

If you've got access to the Internet, check out Batteries Not Included at http://www.mentertainment.com/video/101-202.htm. This site posts reviews of X-rated movies so you can find one that is closest to your taste. Remember that many of the films are awful, with bad acting and no plot, so definitely rent before you buy.

For Her

❤ Wander through the back room at the video store and look at the films they have on display. Don't look and say to yourself, Well, I'll never look that way in a bikini. Of course you won't. Merely look to see what's sexy, what turns men on. Then, if you find one that appeals, even just a little bit, rent it. Go ahead. It's really all right.

For Fun

❤ If you're feeling adventurous, take a trip to a newsstand or video store together and select something to take home. Talk about your choices, not with jealousy, but with an erotic edge. You might say, "Doesn't what they're doing look delightfully naughty?" or "God, I'd love to see you posed on the bed like that!" Or even "Do real people actually do that?" Then take your choice home and giggle. Look through the magazine or watch the video. Relax and let go. Talk about what you see. Voice some of your fears—for example, "Boy, I wish I

139

looked like that without clothes." You'll be surprised at your lover's response. And don't forget to suggest something that looks delightfully naughty. "I would love it if you would touch me like that." It will probably open new lines of communication and stimulate creative activities.

Images on the Internet

On Saturday Night #18, I introduced you to sex on the Internet. If you are skipping around this book and haven't already read that section, I would suggest you begin there, since there are some general guidelines for Net browsing, such as how to use your system and how to protect children from unwanted material.

Erotic images are everywhere on the Web. There are probably more sites offering erotic images than there are copies of the latest issue of *Playboy*. Well, almost, but you get the idea. What's out there? Everything you can imagine.

Movie Sales

You can purchase X-rated films through hundreds of Web sites. Here are just a few:
*   http://www.69redhot.com
*   http://www.adultsexfilms.com
*   http://www.dvdflix.com/dvd/adult_lobby.asp
*   http://www.excaliburfilms.com
*   http://www.stggroup.com

Photos

Most of the X-rated sites you'll find on the Net have one or more pictures of naked bodies. Photographs tend to be slow appearing on your screen and pages with several photos will take from thirty seconds to several minutes to download. Photos consist of lots of colored dots, and the more dots, the better the quality of the picture. But more dots take longer to transmit. Therefore, many sites have what are called "thumbnails," smaller versions of the large pictures. They display lots of tiny pictures, and when you find a tiny photo you would like to look at, click on it and—voilà—the large picture is transmitted to your screen.

Many of the photo sites have music, audios of heavy breathing, or actual dialogue, for which, in most cases, you have to download software that plays the sound. I must admit that I've not downloaded any of these. I'm a bit reticent to put anything on my hard drive that I don't understand, so I will leave this up to you.

Video and Live Sex Shows

Lots of sites have live action or film clips that you can see right on your computer screen. Do they work? I'm sure they do, but again, I've not downloaded the players that enable you to see the action. Are the live feeds actually live? Most of the time, they are. Sex shows in all forms are quite legal in many foreign countries— notably, the Netherlands, so many of the live sex shows come from there. The site merely transmits video of the live shows that are going on all the time. If watching live sex acts excites you, you'll have a large selection to choose from. Here's your opportunity to view anything and everything without going to a strip club. Most of these sites require payment, but if that's what you want, it's worth a few dollars. Just sign up for a short time to see whether it's to your liking or whether, after the first week or so, the thrill wears off.

A note here: Picture sites on the Web tend to appear and disappear rather quickly. One day, you're enjoying photos, and the next day, you click and get a message saying that the site referenced can no longer be parsed, or some such. So rather than annoy you with lists of sites that might no longer exist, I've listed a few link sites from which you can click to whatever sites strikes your fancy. See page 86 or consult the appendix at the back of this book for a listing of those sites.

Amateurs on the Web

There are many individuals and couples who are, at heart, exhibitionists. They get a thrill out of knowing that people are looking at them. Now they have a new and delicious outlet for their energy. They create their own Web sites and post erotic photos of themselves. They are nonprofessionals and take and display their photos for the sheer joy of knowing that someone's looking. Some of the photos have a really professional look; others are really amateur.

There are also sites that post collections of amateur photos, with models and sex acts of all description. In addition, I've seen sites that offer pictures supposedly taken with hidden cameras, showing shots up women's dresses or in changing rooms at clothing stores. Whatever turns you on, I guess, although I shudder at some of these seemingly nonconsensual activities.

Are all the people in these pictures really amateurs, people who don't get paid for their pictures? I doubt it. Who cares? It's the thrill for you that's important, not the folks who posed for the pictures. Certainly, some are really pictures of women and men who enjoy exposing themselves and knowing that folks in all countries of the world are getting a thrill out of seeing their naked bodies. Here are two link sites through which you can find lots of amateur sites.

- http://www.100top.com/amateur/index.html
- http://www.amateur1000.com

Stars

There are hundreds of sites devoted to nude photos of famous movie and TV stars. Many are real, but many more are fakes—just celebrity heads electronically joined to nude bodies. It's almost impossible to tell which is which. But does it matter?

* http://www.nudecelebritystars.com
* http://www.mufflist.com
* http://www.theharem.com

Specialty sites: These are picture sites that cater to specific tastes.

* http://www.fetish1000.com
* http://www.gay1000.com
* http://www.lesbian1000.com
* http://www.palace.com/exchan: Bondage and fetish links.

As you can see, there's something for almost everyone on the Internet. Browsing, either alone to get warmed up or with your partner as a sex activity in and of itself, is a fantastic way to spend an evening.

For Fun

❤️♡ Find a site on the Net that makes your skin tingle and share it with your partner. Look at the images together and use one as a model for the evening. "Let's make love like that" or "How about doing that to me?" or "I'd love to do that to you." Looking at the pictures not only can get you both in the mood but it can also open up lines of communication that will lead to better lovemaking.

143

Saturday Night #30

Catalogs—Looking Is More Than Half the Fun

The catalog business is bigger than ever. There are astounding figures indicating that Americans buy a significant percentage of their holiday merchandise from catalogs. I don't know about you, but my mailbox is filled with slick paper magazines throughout the months of September and October, all vying for my purchasing dollar. Well, the sex industry is no different, and for our purposes, that's the good news. Tonight you're going to make use of all those delicious, sexy catalogs to initiate a night of sensational sex.

Some of the most common of the sex-oriented catalogs are the ones that sell lingerie. But selling lingerie isn't the only thing that these catalogs do. The figures aren't available, but I'm told that more than half the subscribers to Victoria's Secret catalogs are men. And most of them don't buy items; they just look at the pictures. Both Frederick's of Hollywood and Victoria's Secret have made fortunes catering to the lingerie tastes of adults. Now these companies have grown to the extent that they have retail stores in virtually every mall and now their undie ads have begun to appear on network television.

For Her

❤ Let me take a moment to talk about lingerie catalogs and the models who wear the merchandise. Ladies, those women are incredibly gorgeous to begin with, and then their images are retouched. Don't be discouraged. Men love to look at the women in the catalogs, and those in the centerfold of *Playboy,* too, but remember this: You're warm and alive and right there, ready, willing, and able, unlike the two-dimensional versions. Don't compare. If photos get his hormones raging, great. You're the one he's going to make love to.

If you let it, your body image will defeat you before you start looking at catalogs, and that's not only counterproductive, it's downright dumb. We're all imperfect. I'm about fifteen pounds overweight and, at almost sixty, I sag in lots of places, and I do mean *lots.* I've long since ceased thinking how I'd love to be twenty again. Frankly, I'd love to be fifty again. We women constantly torture ourselves with diets, expensive creams and lotions, and strange exercises, just to be what we think our partners want us to be. Remember, you're the one he selected. Think sexy thoughts and you can be so much more than any woman he sees in photos.

For Him

❤ Body image is much more of a problem for women than for men. You guys don't worry about every extra pound and where it's going to show up. We do, and although we try not to be slaves to the way we see ourselves, it happens. It's important that you make your lady feel attractive. Tell her how hot she makes you. Tell her that you love looking at her naked body. She won't believe you the first dozen times you say it, but if you tell her often enough, while making long, luxurious love, eventually she'll start to believe that you think she's sexy and attractive, and that's enough.

For Both of You

♥ Catalogs that sell "adult merchandise" are good not only for use in purchasing items but also for just browsing. As you can imagine, I'm on the mailing list for dozens of catalogs that sell items of all kinds. Ed and I often paw through them just to see what's out there, and we get in the mood that way, just as you will.

What do they sell? You can buy everything from shoes with five-inch heels to tight, short leather skirts, from maid's outfits to twelve-inch shocking-pink dildos. Would you buy those items? Maybe not. However, looking at the pictures, reading the descriptions, and imagining what you would do with the product if you had it is half (or more than half) the fun.

For tonight, get ahold of a catalog. I've listed some 800 numbers here for places that will send you catalogs. Some require a small payment, which will be deducted from your first purchase. I've tried to list only the ones that have been in business for several years and seem reputable, but, as you can imagine, I haven't ordered from every one, so please take a bit of care. Since many of these companies make additional money by selling their mailing lists, you'll get on some *interesting* lists over the next weeks. If you are worried about your children intercepting your mail, you might want to have your catalogs sent to your office, a neighbor's house, or a post office box. Oh, yes, they do come in plain brown wrappers, so there's more danger of them being tossed out with the junk mail than that they'll advertise your bravery to the neighbors or the person who delivers your mail.

Okay, you've gotten a catalog. Now what? For the moment, just let your fingers tiptoe through the pages—together. Phew, it can get a bit embarrassing. Those dreaded knee-jerk reactions. "You wouldn't ever buy that, would you?" "I can't imagine anyone actually doing that." "You've got to be kidding." The truth is, that for everything that anyone sells, there are buyers or the items wouldn't be sold. Your partner, sitting right next to you, might be just the one whose palms are getting sweaty and whose hands are shaking. That's terrific.

As you've done many times before, raise your radar antenna and try to understand what your partner's telling you. Does the photo of the dildo make her shudder? Is that shudder rejection or excitement? Does the photo of the pair of handcuffs make his hands tremble just a bit? Maybe, just maybe, he's telling you something.

How do you find out what really turns your partner on? Try asking, "What do you think that's used for?" or "How do you think that person feels holding that?" You can say, "I think that's kind of wild" or "That looks sort of intriguing." You'll be surprised what you'll find out.

For Fun

❤♡ Give your partner an imaginary fifty-dollar gift certificate that he or she *has* to spend on merchandise from the catalog. "What would you buy?" you ask. If your partner is really reluctant, you start. "I'd probably buy that tube of flavored lubricant. You pick next."

147

For Fun

❤♡Use a picture in the catalog for a jumping-off place for a story. "Maybe he's just gotten a box in the mail from this company. Maybe there's a vibrator inside and he's about to go into the bedroom and help his wife use it. What would happen? I wonder."

Here's another way to play. Give the catalog to your partner to read in private. Ask him or her to circle some item that you can buy as a present; then put the catalog in your dresser drawer.

Just remember to keep the catalogs away from your children. This is private stuff, not for the eyes of the younger folks.

I have some addresses for you, but please beware. When writing this book, I checked all of the phone numbers listed here, but lots of time will have elapsed by the time the book is published, and more may go by before you decide to use the addresses or phone numbers here. Many will have changed, or the stores may have moved. I just checked on the 800 number of a company that used to sell "adult bedroom accessories." When I called, the number belonged to a mortgage company. Hmm. And my list is far from exhaustive. There are dozens of companies appearing and several disappearing each month, so be flexible.

Most of these companies now also have Web sites, and on another Saturday night here, I'll help you let your mouse do the shopping. In case you want to surf the Web, I've listed the Web site addresses for many of the catalog companies, too.

FOR LINGERIE

- Frederick's of Hollywood
  PO Box 229
  Hollywood, CA 90078-0229

1-800-323-9525
http://www.fredericks.com
- Victoria's Secret
  PO Box 16589
  Columbus, OH 43216-6589
  1-800-888-8200
  http://www.victoriassecret.com

FOR TOYS AND SUCH
- Adam and Eve
  PO Box 800
  Carrboro, NC 27510
  1-800-274-0333
  http://www.aeonline.com
- Alisha's Luvtoys
  VMU
  11757 W. Ken Caryl Avenue
  Suite F 210
  Littleton, CO 80127
  1-800-932-7014 (United States only)
  http://www.luvtoys.com
- Eve's Garden
  119 West 57th Street, #420
  New York, NY 10019
  1-800-848-3837
  http://www.evesgarden.com
- Good Vibrations
  938 Howard Street
  Suite 101
  San Francisco, CA 94103
  1-800-289-8423 (Mon.–Sat. 7:00 A.M.–7:00 P.M.—PT)
  http://www.goodvibes.com

- Intimate Treasures (they have not only adult products but also a catalog of catalogs—a real find.)
  PO Box 77902
  San Francisco, CA 94107
  1-415-863-5002
  http://www.intimatetreasures.com
- The Xandria Collection (catalogs cost $2–$5, depending on the content)
  PO Box 319005
  San Francisco, CA 94131-9988
  1-800-242-2823
  http://www.xandria.com

FOR VIDEOS
- Leisure Time Products
  PO Box M827
  Gary, IN 46401-9900
  1-800-874-8960
- VCI
  PO Box 5185
  Willowick, OH 44095
  1-800-886-3410 (11:00 A.M.–9:00 P.M.—ET)

SPECIALTY ITEMS
- Brazen Images (naughty cards, gift wrap, games, erotic chocolates, party supplies, and much more)
  PO Box 731
  Hartsdale, NY 10530-0731
  1-914-949-2605 (leave a message 24 hours a day)
  http://www.brazenimages.com
- DeMars Sexy Footwear, Cypress Footwear, and USA Shoes

and Boots (three interlinked companies specializing in
shoes and boots)
11542 Knott Street
Unit B-7
Garden Grove, CA 92841
1-714-903-2502
http://www.usashoes.com (with links from there to the
other two)

- Dream Dresser (from latex to maid's uniforms, everything
  for playing dress-up)
  PO Box 16158
  Beverly Hills, CA 90209-2158
  1-213-848-3480
  http://www.dreamdresser.com
- Fashion World International (costumes and more)
  9777 Business Park Drive
  Suite C
  Sacramento, CA 95827
  1-916-631-8777
  http://www.fantasyfashion.com
- Leather for Lovers
  PO Box 78550
  San Francisco, CA 94107-8550
  1-415-863-4822
  http://www.voyages.com
- Romantic Fantasy (leather clothing)
  Donnelly Enterprises
  8320 Denise Drive
  Seminole, FL 33777
  1-727-393-9646 (Mon.–Thurs. 7:00 A.M.–10:30 A.M.—ET)
  http://www.jampacked.com

Okay, you've looked at a catalog or browsed a few Web sites, giggled together, and decided to buy something. But what to buy? I have lots of suggestions and a few warnings. Decide on a budget and have a blast. Buy something and let your partner open the present when you have lots of time to play, or pick out the item to buy together. And yes, all items do arrive in plain boxes. The neighbors will never know. Here's what's around to buy.

Lingerie

This is an easy and nonthreatening place to start. Buy some sexy undies, or an outfit to be worn only in the house during private moments. You'll find everything from see-through cat suits and satin corsets to bras with openings over the nipples and crotchless panties. There are also items for men: satin shorts, sexy net tank tops, thong briefs that fit tightly between the buttocks, and pouches that accentuate a man's penis and testicles. Indulge.

Dildos

Dildos come in all shapes, colors, and sizes. There are vaginal ones, ones specifically designed to stimulate the G-spot, ones designed for anal penetration (Saturday Night #50 is devoted to anal sex, so if you're interested in this kind of play, flip pages), and even double-ended ones that stimulate both vagina and anus at the same time. You can buy dildos made of hard plastic or of a softer, rubbery material; ones that you can fill with hot water, or ice cubes; ones that will stimulate the clitoris; ones with simulated testicles; and even ones that glow in the dark or bend to new and unusual shapes. They come alone, or with harnesses so they can be worn. Like every other type of sex toy, they come in all price ranges. You can also buy them in sets with dildos in different shapes.

Vibrators

Like dildos, vibrators come in all shapes and sizes. There are two possible power sources: battery and electric. The battery-powered ones are much more portable, but they tend to be less powerful. With the ones you have to plug in, you're limited by the length of the cord, but they tend to produce stronger vibrations. If you purchase the battery type, check the description so you have the proper size batteries on hand when it arrives. Nothing is more frustrating than opening the package, ready for a good time, and discovering you don't have the right batteries. For the plug-in types, have an extension cord handy, but take care not to electrocute yourself. Never use an electrically powered vibrator in the bathroom, where water might short out the connections, or worse.

Although many people use vibrators during foreplay, don't overlook the delightful fun you can have playing with a vibrator during intercourse. It feels as good on his genitals as on hers. Try pressing a vibrator on her pubic bone so that he can feel the vibrations through her body. There are even specialty products, like clitoral vibrators that a man can wear on his penis and that press against a woman while having intercourse.

Bondage and S/M Equipment

You can indulge to your heart's content with this type of toy (if you're interested in this, you might want to flip ahead to Saturday Night #52.) Manacles, blindfolds, whips, corsets, and G-strings trimmed with chains, rings, hooks, and whatever other doodads suit your fancy can be purchased in leather or latex. You can get wooden paddles, handcuffs, nipple clamps, penis harnesses, and so much more, it's impossible to mention everything.

Dress-up Items

Here again, the sky's the limit. You can get costumes in leather, lace, satin, and latex. There are police outfits, maid's uniforms, leather stretch pants for men and women, thigh-high boots with five-inch heels, and see-through teddies. And on and on.

Movies

A few Saturday nights ago I talked at some length about adult movies. There are so many catalogs and Web sites that sell "adult" movies that it's difficult to sort through them all. My only warning here is to watch how much you spend. General films can be bought at reasonable prices, but those with "specialties" like whipping, same-sex relations, and bondage can get quite pricey. One way to discover what you like is to rent a few first at your video store. See what you like before you shell out good money. Most films are not returnable.

Erection-Prolonging Creams

There are lots of creams, sprays, and lotions that claim to keep the penis erect longer, and many do. They contain an anesthetic, like lidocaine or benzocaine, that numbs the penis to minimize sensations. If you want to keep your erection longer, give it a try.

Lubricants

As we've discussed, no product that contains any petroleum ingredient should be used as a lubricant. Vaseline and baby oil are especially forbidden, both for health and safety reasons.

However, in addition to good old K-Y jelly, every general-merchandise catalog advertises lots of different lubricating products. Read the ingredients carefully before you buy. Slippery Stuff, Aqua Lube, and Astroglide can be found in most catalogs. If you use one type and it gets tacky before you need to use it, get another. Experiment!

Products to Pleasure Men

There are artificial vaginas and inflatable toys with openings at strategic places, vibrating devices of all shapes, cock rings that keep the penis erect by shutting off the return of blood, and sleeves that fit over the penis to increase sensation during masturbation. There's bound to be something to please him.

Aphrodisiacs

Take care here. There are no real aphrodisiacs, at least the way you want to think of them. Many products, however, "guarantee to make her (or him) yours." Try to collect on such a guarantee. Yeah, right! Drugs of any kind, from Spanish fly and yohimbine to cocaine, are extremely dangerous, and if they don't injure you, they often have the opposite effect from the one you want. A word to the wise: *Don't.* At best, they are a waste of money. At worst, they can leave you impotent or sterile.

Phew. There's so much, you won't know where to begin. Just begin somewhere. Next week, we'll enjoy a special Saturday night, the one when we open the package.

Saturday Night # 31

Me? Actually Order Something?

ow that you've selected something to buy, you're ready to place an order. I can hear you now. "Me? Actually call one of *those* companies?" Of course, you can always send the order in by mail or fax, but you really can call. Do it tonight.

I remember the first time I actually ordered something from a catalog. A phone order seemed efficient, but I was a wreck. I wanted to buy a present for Ed and me to play with, a collection consisting of three dildos in different shapes. In addition to just playing, I was really curious as to whether the different shapes would change the sensations. The catalog contained an 800 number, and I was reasonably sure the company involved was reliable. But I couldn't make the call. I thought, How am I going to tell some phone operator that I want to buy dildos? She'll know for sure that I'm kinky. She'll ask me embarrassing questions about my sex life. She'll *know*.

It took me days before I felt brave enough to pick up the phone and dial. Well, I was greeted on the phone by a professional order clerk who efficiently took all my information and couldn't have cared less about my sex life. She was just doing her job. Remember, the companies are in business to make money, so if they make ordering uncomfortable, and lose a paying customer, they won't survive for long.

So select something you'd like to buy. Keep it simple for the first time—maybe just a selection of condoms or some massage oil. Some of the catalogs have minimum dollar amounts, so keep your order just above that amount. Be brave and pick up the phone, or, if you're not feeling adventurous, fill out the order form and mail or fax it in.

As you did when you thought about requesting a catalog, you might want to consider where to have your order sent. If you've got curious children, you don't want strange boxes to arrive at your door. "What's in the package, Dad?" your child will ask, and what will you answer? So you might want to have your order shipped to a friend, to your office, or a post office box. Renting a post office box is a small price to pay for your privacy.

When the package arrives, make a Saturday night of it. Relax, have a beer, and present your partner with your surprise gift. Open the box together. You might find that he or she is deliciously horrified. "You didn't really spend money on that, did you?" Don't be discouraged. Think about how you might have reacted under the same circumstances. Your first sex toy, whatever it may be, really hits a nerve, and that's both the good and bad news. It's a touchy moment, so try really hard, both of you, to think before you speak, and realize that this is a bit of a surprise. But it's an arousing one, too.

Maybe the item you bought touches you both in a wonderful spot. That's perfect. Now's the time for an adventurous evening of sex play, and the newness will stimulate all kinds of creative thoughts and feelings, so go with them and frolic.

157

You might also find that what you ordered didn't turn out to be what you thought, or doesn't work. I remember buying a set of ben wha balls, metal spheres that a woman inserts into her vaginal channel to cause sexual stimulation. I'd read stories about women who had inserted them and become instantly aroused. Hmm. Well, I inserted them and waited. Nothing. I found that they had no effect at all. I stood up and walked around. One fell out. Maybe I wasn't using them correctly, but I couldn't think of anything else to do with them. I think they are still at the bottom of our toy bag. However, thinking about the sex play that would ensue had excited both Ed and me, and we had a delicious evening anyway.

Remember that the most powerful erogenous zone is the mind, and if the toy you've purchased doesn't excite the body as you expected it to, the mere act of opening the box will arouse your libido.

As you get more experienced at ordering, you might want to get more adventurous, as well. Next week, we'll click around on the Internet. For tonight, get brave and actually order something from that catalog. Just do it, no matter how ridiculous it feels. You'll be amazed and delighted when you receive your new toy and play together.

For Fun

❤♡ Let's say the package arrives on Thursday. Make your lover impatient for Saturday night by teasing with it. "I ordered something from a toy catalog and the package arrived today. But you can't open it until Saturday night." Remember that anticipation is half the fun. Maybe you can allow him or her one guess a night until the great unveiling.

Saturday Night #32

Let Your Mouse Do the Shopping

dult business is flourishing on the Internet. There are literally hundreds of sites that sell adult merchandise. You can begin on my Web site at http://www.joanelloyd.com and use my list of links to begin browsing. Follow your libido and click around. You'll find everything for sale, and I do mean everything.

Like looking through catalogs, surfing the Net can be a really arousing experience. You'll see products of all kinds and if you and your partner are sitting side by side at the keyboard, you can slip in little suggestions like, "You know I'd love to try something like that. How about you?" Try to listen through the automatic "I couldn't possibly" and hear the "Oooh, that's looks soo sexy, but I couldn't really admit it."

Ordering items can be really simple. A click-click here and a click-click there, a credit card number and you've done it. Soon the item or items will arrive and the fun will start.

159

In the Saturday night devoted to ordering from catalogs, I listed many companies that are both catalog and on-line resources. Here are a few places that specialize in on-line sales, have specialty items, or whose catalogs are expensive.

Several sites call themselves Sex Malls and have collected lots of "stores" you can click to that sell everything from toys and videos to lingerie, fetish items, photos, books, and erotic greeting cards. Try:

- http://www.pricebusters.com
- http://www.sexmall.com
- http://www.tcmd.com/app/index.html

And here are a few sites, in addition to those already mentioned, that specialize in toys:

- http://www.1adultsextoystore.com
- http://www.a-romantic.com: A soft-core site that might be a good place to begin.
- http://www.adultatrium.com
- http://www.bedroomsports.com: A good on-line only store.
- http://www.castlesuperstore.com: Castle Superstores is an on-line store that also has ten physical locations throughout the U.S. Their site also has a huge link list including many sex search engines and lots of erotica sites.
- http://www.eroticsextoys.com
- http://www.thepleasurechest.com
- http://www.sextoyshoppers.com

Here are two fun sites that specialize in erotic games:

- http://www.erotic-games.com: They have over two hundred down-loadable adult games and screensavers.
- http://www.firstfantasies.com: This site has imaginative kits for fantasy role-playing and has to be visited to be appreciated.

Finally, here are a few that just didn't fit anywhere else but are really worth a visit:

- http://www.bodyandbath.mb.ca: Bath products such as oils, creams, soaps, and bath salts.
- http://www.csense.com—Condom Sense is a gentle site with everything from valuable information to gag gifts. They can also be reached at 1-888-70CONDOM from 9:00 A.M.– 5:00 P.M. PT.
- http://www.nonpiercingjewelry.com
- http://www.freelove.com: Sex, hard-core jigsaw puzzles, and on-line games.
- http://www.euromode.com/rp/index.htm: A hot assortment of large-size lingerie (1X to 4X).

Now buy something. Do it! I know it feels silly and a bit risky, but nothing ventured, nothing gained. And maybe your partner would like to purchase something but is even more reluctant than you are. Okay, be the brave one. Click, click, have some fun.

For Fun

♥♡ Maybe your new toy lends itself to this idea. Surprise your partner with, "I got a package today that contained something I ordered from a sexy catalog. Want to frisk me and see where I hid it?"

For Fun

♥♡ Print out a picture of what you've purchased and jot down the date you expect it to arrive. Then wrap your partner's toothbrush with it and let your lover anticipate the big night.

161

Saturday Night #33

How to Touch Each Other

You have already learned how your partner gives himself or herself pleasure. Tonight, it's time to learn how you can use your hands to give your partner increased erotic enjoyment.

As with everything else, your partner is your best guide. His or her moans, groans, sighs, and movements will be your best indication of what's giving pleasure. But there are certain basics that you can try. Remember, nothing works for everyone, and nothing works all the time. Part of the pleasure of touching is variation. Do something today, and then something quite different tomorrow. That doesn't mean you have to invent new things every day. Far from it. But it's sort of like food. You might love a big juicy steak, but you wouldn't want to eat one every night for the rest of your life. You'd love the occasional bowl of spaghetti or a Big Mac. So go back to something you two enjoyed a month ago, or a week ago. Boredom and predictability are the slow death of great sex.

For Him

❤ Where does she like to be touched? She's shown you where she is sensitive in her vaginal area, but she really likes to be touched everywhere. Men usually like to "get to it." Women like to play. So take your time. Kiss—all over. Stroke with the tips of your fingers. Begin everywhere but those erogenous zones. Stroke her forehead, her eyes, her neck. Run your fingers through her hair. You'd be amazed at how sensitive the scalp really is. Run your fingers lightly over the insides of her arms, the tops of her shoulders. Take a moment. Remember that she heats up slowly, so take your time, but enjoy the journey.

About breasts. Too many men think the only part of a woman's breast that's sensitive and arousing is the nipple area. Not so. All the flesh on a woman's breast is really delicate, and it feels wonderful to be stroked softly, fingers swirling toward the areola, the darker area, but not quite reaching it. Tease. Tempt. That's what it's all about. She'll tell you with her movements how delectable it is.

Touching a woman's nipple is extremely exciting. Nipples are made of erectile tissue, similar to a man's penis, and when aroused, nipples tighten and form tight buds. That can be a wonderful indicator that what you're doing is pleasing. For me, from lots of years of tight bras and the friction of clothing, my nipples aren't terribly sensitive to light touches. I need stronger pressure to feel anything. Pinching lightly or rolling the nipple between index finger and thumb feels great. But, as with anything else, ask your partner whether you're doing things too hard or too softly.

Stroking lower can be wonderful or, for women like me, can take a bit of care. I'm ticklish, and I hate being tickled. Stroking my belly and ribs must be done with a firm touch, if at all. It's not that laughter has no place in the bedroom. Quite the contrary. But for

163

women who don't enjoy being tickled, it's an irritant. There are some women, however, who really enjoy being tickled, and for whom tickling can even be a prelude to sex. If your lover's one of those, go for it.

You're getting nearer the genital area now. Stroke the insides of her thighs, the backs of her knees, always getting closer to her vagina and clitoris, but not quite there yet. Remember, you're teasing. Brush your fingers lightly over her pubic hair, just touching the tips of the hairs slightly.

Once her hips are urging you toward her center, begin by exploring. You might know her body well, but wetting a finger, parting the outer lips, slowly delving into every crevice feels fantastic. Take your time and don't aim for the clitoris or the vagina yet. Make love to her body as she heats and don't ignore those areas you already stroked. They still feel fantastic.

By now, she should be moaning and very wet. With almost all premenopausal women, natural lubrication is a prelude to intercourse. If a woman's not wet yet, she's probably not really excited. For postmenopausal women, this isn't necessarily true, since the lack of hormones sometimes leads to vaginal dryness. You're the best judge of whether she's really hot now or not. If you're not sure, ask. "Oh, baby, I want to slide my fingers inside of you. Would that feel good?" She'll tell you if she's ready. If not, take a bit more time to tease. If she's ready and not wet, use a bit of commercial lubricant. Never try to put your finger or your penis into a dry vagina. It's not going to be comfortable for either of you.

Try lightly squeezing her outer or inner lips between the pads of your index finger and thumb or pulling on them slightly. Does she arch her back? Great. If she pulls away, do something else. Take care not to catch her pubic hairs or scratch her with an errant fingernail. I've had both done to me, and it momentarily squashes a good mood. You can hope she'll tell you but some women don't want to say anything. So do everything you can to encourage communication and be careful.

Whisper to her all the while. Tell her how sexy she is, how hot she's making you. Afraid that her man is bored or that his hands are getting tired, many women will rush, at the expense of their own pleasure. Let her know that you're enjoying pleasuring her and that her enjoyment is arousing you.

When touching a woman's clitoris, stroke with a well-lubricated finger, touching around the sides and in the valleys, rather than directly on the top. For most women, this is as exciting as touching the clitoris itself, or even more so, since rubbing the top of the clitoris can sometimes be "too much." And don't concentrate in any one place, even on the clitoris. Touch there and then touch somewhere else. Use your other hand to stroke, pinch, tweak, and play with other parts of her body.

Finger penetration should be attempted only when a woman's already aroused and wet. Slowly insert one finger, sliding partway in, then pulling out, each time moving slightly deeper. If she gives indication she wants more, a second and even a third finger can be added.

Thrusting with your fingers, imitating the thrusts of intercourse, is one of the most exciting sensations for a woman. Sometimes a woman wants to be "fucked" hard, with your hand really slamming against her body. Do it hard if she asks, but remember that harder isn't necessarily faster. Don't rush. If she yells, "More!" check to see whether she wants you to insert another finger, move faster, or press harder. The combination of clitoral stimulation and finger penetration can lead to a strong orgasm. Remember not to forget the rest of her body while you're doing this. You might try placing the heel of your other hand on her lower abdomen while your fingers are inside. That can create a delicious sensation for her, and you can actually feel the clenching of her muscles as she comes.

About the G-spot. Yes, it exists. Almost every expert has now discovered that there is an area of sensitive tissue in the vaginal canal, about two inches above (deeper inside than) the ridge of bone, on the front, or belly, side of the channel. Often it will feel thick or ridged. For a woman like me, who wore a diaphragm for many years, it can be difficult or even impossible to find, but the fun's in the looking anyway. Once you find it—which is easiest with a crooked finger, making a sort of "come here" motion—rhythmically rubbing that spot leads to what some women say is a different kind of orgasm. Or try press and release, press and release, as if you're pressing an elevator button.

Try touching the perineum, the area between the vaginal opening and the anus, or even touch the anal opening itself. However, if you touch the anus, don't touch the vagina again without washing your hands. If you want to touch the anus, however briefly, you might try slipping a condom on your finger or wearing some latex gloves, which can cause a delicious feeling, and they are easy to remove. If you're considering anal penetration, see Saturday Night #50 and read at length about anal sex.

At this point, if you want to play with a toy, a vibrator or dildo inserted into the channel can push a woman still higher. Or touch the end or side of the clitoris with a vibrator. Take your time and experiment.

For Her

❤♡Touching a man is different from touching a woman, and hooray for that. That means, however, that we, too, have to learn.

While a woman likes to be teased and played with, most men want more direct action. Back rubs, kissing, and stroking are fine, but usually they should be of limited duration. Once aroused, a man gets most pleasure from hands on his penis. Wrap your fingers around his erect member and stroke firmly from tip to base. You will probably need some form of lubrication, like the seminal fluid that might already be leaking from the tip, or a commercial lubricant. Or use the heel of your hand to trap his penis between your hand and his belly, rubbing along its length from base to tip, then back down to the base again.

You can grasp the penis with one hand at the tip and slide the fist down to the base. As one hand reaches the base and releases, the other grasps the tip and slides up again, repeating with alternate hands. You can also try this in the opposite direction, from base to tip. Or you can tighten the fist over the head of the penis so it has to fight to penetrate. As the head finally pushes through the opening, the other hand can grasp and continue the same thing. This can give the sensation of penetrating a tight, infinitely long vagina.

Pulling the skin tightly over the penis increases the sensitivity. Move from head to base, pulling the skin as you go. Then use the other hand to squeeze, rub, or even corkscrew over the end. Or you can gently twist the head of the penis as if you're trying to turn a doorknob. You can form a tight ring around the base of his penis with your index finger and thumb in an O shape. If held tightly, at the base, your fingers will form a cock ring, which prevents the return flow of blood, making the erection harder and longer-lasting. As with everything, let his level of excitement be your guide.

A man's testicles are sensitive and a source of pleasure, too. Cupping the balls and lightly squeezing or tickling the sac can be very exciting. Then you can slide one or two fingers backward, toward the anal area, massaging his sensitive perineum. You can also touch the anus itself without worry of infection. Of course, don't touch your own vaginal tissues without washing your hands first.

Although I cover anal sex in some detail in the last section, a word might be in order here about a man's prostate. If you insert a well-lubricated finger, covered with a condom or latex glove, into his anus about one and a half to two inches, you'll find a dome-shaped gland on the front or belly side. Rubbing it can be intensely pleasurable for a man.

For Both of You

❤♡Don't forget to add props to your touching. Put a satin scarf between your hand and his erection or rub it with a furry mitten. Put on a latex glove or rub her clitoris with cold lubricant for a change of sensation.

Whether you take turns touching each other or try to do it at the same time, enjoy each other. Talk dirty. Create fantasies. Keep raising the heat level until you fall on each other like animals, or climax without intercourse. What a great way to spend a Saturday night.

Saturday Night #34

Erotic Beginnings
—Part 3

These tales center around making love with someone who's less knowledgeable about the ways of good sex. Haven't you ever wanted to teach someone about the joys of great lovemaking? Or have you wanted to be taught? Read on.

THE WEDDING NIGHT

Alice and Ted had spent considerable time together between their engagement and their wedding, but, as Ted thought back on it now, they had seldom been alone. Alice came from a huge family and it had been almost impossible to separate her from one or another of her brothers, sisters, cousins, aunts. . . . Her relatives were too numerous to count, and too confusing to keep

169

track of. But they had gotten married that afternoon, and were finally alone on their wedding night.

Ted, still dressed in his tuxedo, looked around the sitting room of the suite at the Plaza Hotel. They were going to be in New York for a week, a gift from a group of Alice's relatives. "Darling," he called softly toward the closed bedroom door, "are you ready?"

"I guess," came the soft voice, and he grinned. They had necked and petted but hadn't made love as yet. He knew it would be wonderful, though. And he was hungry to enjoy his new wife for the first time.

He opened the door wide and saw the wonderful woman he had married. She was standing in the middle of the room, dressed in a virginal white lace negligee and dressing gown set. Her hair hung loose around the lovely face Ted knew so well, but her expression puzzled him. She looked for all the world like a lamb being led to the slaughter. "Darling," he said, truly confused, "you look so miserable. What's wrong?"

When she remained silent, he crossed the room and placed a hand on each of her trembling shoulders. "Tell me, love. What's so terrible?"

Her lower lip quivering, she said, "We never . . ."

"That makes this all the more wonderful. I wanted to make love to you so many times, but there was never an opportunity. Now we can be together here, in private, just you and me."

"But . . . I mean . . . I never . . ." She burst into tears.

Slowly, understanding dawned. "Do you mean to say that you have never made love? To anyone?" When he saw her nod, he folded her into his arms. "Oh, love, how . . ."

"My parents felt they were protecting all of us from the evil in this world. They were very strict."

"I knew that, but I never thought they had succeeded."

"They didn't entirely. My sister Marianne sneaks out and runs around with all the boys. She has told me how wonderful making love is." Though her lower lip trembled, she smiled. "From the frequency with which she disappears after we all are supposed to be asleep, I assume she enjoys it a lot. But . . ."

Ted stroked Alice's long hair, then cupped her chin and turned her face up to look at him. "Are you afraid?"

"A little. I know what happens, of course, but still . . . I know it hurts."

"Only for a moment. I promise. If you want me to stop, all you have to do is tell me and I will. Do you understand that?"

The corners of her mouth curved upward a tiny bit. "Yes. I also know how much I love you." She leaned into his palm and pressed his hand against her face.

"Then there's nothing for you to be afraid of." Ted stood, holding Alice with one arm while the fingers of his other hand traced the softness of her cheek, the firmness of her brow, the cleft in her chin. He tangled his hands in her long hair and rubbed her scalp. "So lovely," he purred.

Alice pressed her face against his body and felt the words rumble deep in his chest. She felt his hand press the small of her back against the hard length of his body and she reflexively flattened her palms against the front of his dress shirt. She was still nervous, but somewhere a tiny voice told her that it was going to be all right. She turned her face toward her new husband.

Barry's Education

Barry was bored. He was home for the three-week break before his last semester in college and everyone was gone. His mother had apologized profusely, but she hadn't been able to pass up the opportunity to join his father on a business trip to

171

Las Vegas for the long weekend, and both his sisters had left right after Christmas to visit schoolmates. Barry hadn't been very popular in high school, so friends were few and far between, and even the few he had were off doing something without him.

In the last few days, he had been to several movies, watched more TV than he had in the past several years, and played so many hours of computer games that his fingers were getting sore. He had roamed the Internet, bopping into chat rooms, trying to connect with someone, if only for a few minutes' diversion. He had even ventured into a few X-rated rooms, hoping for some stimulation.

God, he wanted to get laid.

Sex. He'd had a bit during his years at State, but, if he was being totally truthful, not much. He just wasn't good with girls. Well, he was okay with the friendly part, but when the going got sexual, he whimped out. He wasn't good at it, and he thought he probably would never be.

When the doorbell rang, he loped down the stairs, delighted at the prospect of any kind of distraction. He opened the door wide and was greeted by an amazing smile, and a large apple pie. "Mrs. Kingsley, how nice to see you." The Kingsleys and Barry's family had been neighbors since Barry and Pete Kingsley had been in Little League together, and after her divorce, Mrs. Kingsley had continued to live in the house down the block.

"Barry, it's so good to see you. I heard you were home from school and I've been waiting for you to come visit me."

Strange, Barry thought. Visit *her?* "I was planning on visiting this coming weekend. Is Pete around?"

"He might be home next weekend. He works in the city now, you know."

"No, I didn't."

She pointedly stared at the door. "Well, are we going to stand out here all evening?"

Barry was suddenly aware that he was blocking the doorway. "Sorry." He stepped back. "Come on in, Mrs. Kingsley."

"Thanks," she said, passing him, her subtle perfume filling his nostrils, "and make it Ronnie." She placed a light kiss on his cheek, smiling up at him with a gleam in her eye.

Barry cleared his throat. "Okay. Can I take your coat?"

He quickly put Ronnie's coat in the closet and they moved into the kitchen. Ronnie put the pie on the counter. "I knew everyone was away, so I thought you might be hungry." With a strange expression on her face, she efficiently put on a pot of coffee and cut two slices of the pie. As they ate, they exchanged gossip about all the people they both knew in the neighborhood.

"How are things at school, dear?" Ronnie asked.

Barry began to tell her about his classes, but she interrupted. "I guess what I really meant was, how's your love life?"

"My love life?" Barry took a closer look at Mrs. Kingsley. She was fairly attractive, with great brown eyes and curly brown hair. As she licked her lips, his gaze was riveted on her generous mouth.

"Yes," she said, a slight smile forming. "Do you have a steady girlfriend?"

"Not right now," he said, reluctant to tell her he hadn't had a date since before Thanksgiving.

"Do you get enough?"

Barry was confused. "Enough what?"

Ronnie laughed, the sound deep in her throat. "You know. Do you get enough? A nice-looking guy like you should get lots. I'll bet you have girls begging for it every weekend."

Barry was stunned, and speechless. How had the conversation turned so quickly to sex?

Ronnie stood up, walked behind Barry's chair, and put her hands on his shoulders, kneading his flesh. "I mean, I'll bet you know all the tricks. You young studs can go for hours, then be ready again in minutes."

Barry was aware of how ready he was right now. He hunched over, not willing to let his neighbor see how she'd excited him. Suddenly, he felt her lips on his neck. "You know I feel just like Mrs. Robinson in that movie," she purred. "You know the one I mean?"

Swallowing hard, Barry pictured Anne Bancroft in *The Graduate,* her leg up on that chair. Ronnie was wearing the same expression. "Yes."

"We have this empty house and, well, I'll bet there's a lot we can teach each other."

"I don't think I can teach you much," Barry blurted out.

"Well how about if I teach you?"

Barry swallowed again. "Yeah," he croaked. "Yeah, how about that."

THE PROSTITUTE

Mark was watching television in his living room at about six o'clock one evening when the doorbell rang. "Who's selling what?" he grumbled, climbing out of his lounge chair. "Coming," he yelled as the bell chimed again. He felt for his wallet, ready to shell out a few bucks for Girl Scout cookies.

He opened the door and took a step back to admire the woman who stood there. She was tall, probably five foot eight or nine, with a head full of unruly bright red curls, full red lips, and eyes the color of spring moss. She was wearing an evening dress that looked as if it had been spun from pure silver and it clung to every curve of her slender body. Mark took a shuddering breath and realized that he had a hard-on that wasn't going to let him sleep well that evening. He shook his head slightly. The woman had obviously knocked on the wrong door, more's the pity. "Can I help you?" he asked, trying to control the quaver in his voice.

"Are you Mark Cooper?"

Startled, Mark said, "Yes. What can I do for you?" Had she really come to see him?

"It's what I can do for you," she said, her voice soft and musical. "May I come in?"

As Mark stood aside, the woman walked gracefully into the living room and perched on the edge of an overstuffed chair. "My name is Melody and I have a message for you from"—she pulled a slip of paper from her pocketbook—"Ben, Don, and Paul at your office."

Oh God, he thought, I'm being set up for some goofy practical joke. Those three are impossible.

"'It's been three months since Lynn,'" Melody read, "'and it's time for you to get back into things. Here's something to get into. We love you.'" Melody put the slip of paper back into her purse and smiled. "It sounds like you have some really good friends."

"I guess," Mark said, unable to utter anything more. What could the guys be thinking, sending him a hooker?

"I can tell you're embarrassed, and maybe your friends' choice of a gift wasn't the best, but they obviously meant well. Are they right?"

Mark swallowed and clenched his fists against his thighs. "Right about what?"

"That it's time to get back into the world. I gather you broke up with Lynn three months ago."

"Actually, she dumped me." Now why had he admitted that? He hadn't come to terms with it in his own mind.

"Her loss," Melody said softly. Then a broad grin lit up her elfin

175

face. "And my gain. I'm paid for through tomorrow morning, so why don't we just make the best of it. How about we go out for a drink?"

Out. That sounded so much less threatening than staying in his messy living room. Then he looked at her dress. There was no place he could take someone in an evening dress that looked like that.

"Yeah, right," she said, looking down. "I'm sorry. I didn't know exactly what to wear. But I'm really starved. Have you had dinner?"

Taken aback by the sudden shift of topic, Mark answered, "No. I was going to have pizza."

"Great. Can we call out for something? Do you like pepperoni? How about extra cheese?" When he nodded, mute, she continued, "Why don't you call it in while I change?" She disappeared into the back of the apartment.

Change? Since Mark did it several nights a week, it took very little thought to call Vinny's and order a large pie with pepperoni and extra cheese.

A few moments later, when Melody walked out of the bedroom, Mark gasped. She had removed the silvery dress she had been wearing and had put on one of his dress shirts. She was still wearing her silver high-heeled sandals and silver stockings, and he could see quite a bit of those stockings as his gaze traveled up her long legs. He couldn't help wondering what she had on underneath, and his body reacted to the erotic images his mind conjured up.

As she settled on the sofa, Melody said, "We've got all night. Why don't we just chat for a while and wait for the pizza?"

Chat. Right. Suddenly, all he could think about was what he would find if he slid his hand up the inside of her thigh. Okay, guys, he said mentally to his friends, you've got me. What the hell . . .

I hope you're enjoying these fantasy beginnings, and using them to stimulate evenings of creative lovemaking. For a fourth evening of erotic beginnings, turn to Saturday Night #47.

Saturday Night #35

Making Love Outdoors

onight's lovemaking idea might be difficult for many of you to act upon, but with some creative thinking, you just might pull it off. Have you ever dreamed about making love outdoors, the soft breeze caressing your heated bodies, the sounds of the night loud in your ears, the smell of a campfire or salt air all around you? Most of us have, but few of us have ever carried it through.

A number of years ago, I lived in a house with a balcony off the bedroom. The small porch had been constructed over the garage, and I frequently sunbathed out there or just relaxed in a lawn chair and read. Occasionally, I thought about making love on that balcony, but it was just possible for someone driving by, if he looked up my driveway, to see the porch and me sitting up there. I don't think anyone ever looked, but it was possible.

One evening, Ed and I went up to the bedroom. The door to

the balcony was open and a warm breeze billowed the light curtains. "I'd love to make love out there," Ed said.

"Me, too. But it's a bit too public for me."

"It's almost completely dark. If we turn out all the lights, no one will be able to see."

"But it will be really buggy," I answered, ever practical and a bit reluctant to risk even the minute chance we might be seen.

The light in Ed's eyes changed my mind. Together, we went outside and let nature take its course. At one point, the headlights of a car shone up the driveway and someone drove out of the driveway across the street. I will admit that I found the possibility of being observed both terrifying and exciting. The evening was wonderful, and we repeated the experience several times, until the house was sold. Unfortunately, my condo doesn't lend itself to outdoor frolicking.

The point is, making love outdoors can be delicious. You don't even have to consummate the relationship, just use Mother Nature to heat things up. Here are a few ideas on how to make this happen.

At the Beach

Find a secluded spot and neck. You don't even have to remove your bathing suits; just kiss and touch and fondle. If someone sees what you're doing, who cares? You're entitled. Just don't embarrass anyone else, and try not to be carried away where children might get curious.

A Walk in the Park

She can dress in a loose, flowing skirt and wear no undies. The two of you can take a walk in the park or along a country road.

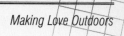

Find a quiet spot where she can spread her skirt and sit down, her hot skin against a cool stone or some prickly grass or an icy streambed. Take care to examine what she's sitting on for hazards. If you like, carry a large kerchief or a thin kitchen towel to spread beneath her bare bottom. Then talk about sensations. Feel!

The Swimming Pool

Nighttime swims are delightfully conducive to love play. If you have a place where you can skinny-dip, great. If not, even with bathing suits on, you can touch beneath the water and no one can see what you're doing. If you're feeling brave, have her remove just the bottom half of her bathing suit and have him take off his trunks. Yes, you can make love beneath the water, but it's a bit of a challenge. I have done it several times in some friends' pool, but the buoyancy makes it a lot bouncier and more difficult to hang on without dunking. Not only was it sexy and hot; it was fun, causing several bouts of giggles. If you don't have a large pool, a small kiddie pool will do on a hot summer night.

Fire Escapes

Do you dare? Those of you who are city folks might want to be really adventurous one evening and spread blankets on the fire escape and make love out there. Take extreme care to be silent, a really sexy addition to this activity. "No screaming, darling. Someone will hear us and look up."

A Cabin in the Deep Woods

Not many of us have the luxury of a place like this, but occasionally there are motels with cabins off to themselves. If you're

179

lucky, you can locate someplace where you can actually play outside, nude, in the sunlight or moonlight, with no one the wiser. Have you ever felt the sun on your secret places? The first time I sunbathed nude, I found the feel of the sun's heat on my private parts surprisingly exciting. Actually, I still do.

In the Car

The next best thing to making love outdoors is making love in the car with all the windows open. You can find that necking spot you used to use, or just park in your own driveway, but be sure to open all the car windows and enjoy the outdoors. This can be erotic in the middle of the winter if you keep the engine running, the heater on full blast, and feel the cold air coming in the window. If it's snowing, all the better.

In the Bedroom

It sounds like a contradiction—making love outdoors in the bedroom. But you can bring some of the same outdoor excitement inside. Get undressed, turn off all the lights, and then open all the windows and turn off the heat or air conditioning. Fill the room with the outside. Listen to the noises, enjoy the fragrances, feel the heat or the cold. If it's summer, let your body sweat a bit and enjoy the feel of your slippery, bare skin. If it's winter, snuggle under the quilt. Cuddle and rub each other to keep warm, naked flesh against naked flesh. You'll heat up very quickly.

The theme for tonight is to think creatively, to bring the exotic thrill of the outdoors into your lovemaking.

Saturday Night #36

A Road Map for the Evening

*H*ere's a neat way to help your partner know exactly what you want the evening to become. Make your lover a detailed list of exactly what to do, and when. It might read like this:

For Her

John, darling,

Tonight I want you to do the following. Go out and buy a bottle of red wine—your choice. Then stop at the supermarket and get a tin of smoked oysters, a jar of olives, a can of asparagus spears—you know, the long, thick ones with the delicious juice—and a bunch of grapes. We can peel them together later.

When you get to the corner of Oak and Maple, pull over and remove

181

your tie. At the next corner, take off your shoes, socks, and belt. Park in the garage, collect all your things, and come inside. Leave your tie, belt, socks, and shoes beside the door and go into the kitchen. Open the wine and put it, two glasses, and the rest of the goodies on a tray.

Remove your shirt. You know how sexy I think you look in just your suit pants. Maybe you should unzip your pants, too.

I'll be waiting in the bedroom.

For Him

Dearest Mary,

Tonight, I want to play with you. I called my folks and they can take the kids overnight. They'll give them dinner, so you can take them over there at about five. Then take a long, hot bubble bath. Use the lavender scent you know I love. Put on that mood-music record we like and light a few candles in the bedroom.

Wait for me in bed, dressed in that cute baby-doll pajama set you got last Christmas. The top only.

I'm bringing home dinner—champagne and sandwiches. We can drink the champagne first and the sandwiches will keep until much later.

For Her

John, darling,

I just thought I'd let you know about tonight. I got tickets for the basketball game, but I'll be tied up all day, so I'll have to meet you at the main entrance about 7:15. You know how chilly that stadium is, so bring a blanket that we can spread over our laps. Of course, since I bought the tickets, I reserve the right to play with you beneath the covers, so be prepared.

For Him

Mary, my love,

In the box with this note, you'll find a pair of handcuffs. Right before you leave the office to meet me for dinner, I want you to put one cuff on your right wrist. You can try to arrange it so the other doesn't show—do your best. I want you to get on the subway and ride home thinking about what we're going to do when you get home. I want to think that someone riding in the subway car with you will be able to see that cuff and will guess what makes you hungry.

You can vary the subject matter as much as you like, but make it really explicit and sexy. The more details you can add, the better. Do you want her in a particularly sexy position? Do you want him to dress in something outrageous? Why not?

If you're into more exotic activities, you might want her to wait for you on her knees with her hands behind her back, or he might tie on a blindfold and lie naked, facedown, on the living room floor.

For Fun

Purchase a magazine with really explicit stories and have your partner read one before the evening begins; then suggest that he or she mimic the activities. There are lots of letter-format magazines available on the newsstand that have such explicit stories. If you want to get more adventurous, try *Variations,* published by *Penthouse.* If you can't get it in your town, see whether a friend in a large city can mail you a copy. It's worth it. If you two have a great evening, a fantastic gift might be a subscription to the magazine in question.

183

You can also use a picture you found in a magazine or on the Internet. Print or tear it out; then tell your partner to be wearing an outfit like the model is wearing, and to wait for you in the exact position as that in the photo. You might even buy the appropriate clothing.

Remember, the idea is anticipation. Tease throughout the day. It makes the evening all the sweeter.

Saturday Night #37

Just Hold Very Still

During lovemaking, both partners are usually quite active, and that's as it should be, each an equal participant in the fun and games. Sometimes, however, it can be really erotic if one partner is totally passive, holding completely still while delicious things are being done to his or her body. It can begin with a discussion about something different for this evening, or it can happen in a flash, just when things are "getting good." Let's look at each.

At the start of this Saturday evening, one partner can mention that he or she would like to "take charge." "Honey, how about letting me do everything to you while you just lie perfectly still?" The other might ask, "What do you mean?" Then say, "Just that I'd like you to put your hands at your sides and do nothing. Don't touch, kiss, or even change positions unless I ask you to." Usually, your partner will shrug at this point, with no clear idea of what's going to happen, and say, "Okay." That's all there is to that part. Then the fun begins.

Or, in the middle of lovemaking, you can suddenly say, "I want you to hold very still while I play. I promise it will be worth your while. Lie quietly, with your hands above your head, and don't move. Even a little bit."

Then begin teasing. That's the most delicious part of this.

For Her

♥♡Straddle his chest and wave your breasts in his face. He might want to kiss and grab, but he's not allowed. Rub your tight nipples over his face and chest. Hold one of his hands between your breasts, then press them together, trapping his fingers. Or, for a singular thrill, trap his erection between them. Stroke his penis or testicles ever so softly with your fingertips. Have you ever wanted to lick him but never had the courage? This is when you can, and then move on if you don't like it. Because, of course, he can't move.

For Him

♥♡Kiss, suck, and lick all the places that you know drive her crazy. If she starts to move, remind her of your agreement. "You're supposed to hold very still, remember?" Rub your erect penis over her fingers. Of course she can't hold you. Does she like being tickled? Touch her ticklish parts with a feather or brush them with the corner of the sheet. Be sure to take your time. The more "tortured" she is, wanting to consummate things, the better.

For Both of You

♥♡When things get really hot, it's natural for hips to move, toes to curl, and knees to bend. It's also natural for hands to reach out. Here comes the fun part. Remind your lover that movement is still not permitted. "Hold still!" It can drive one really crazy to want but not be able to have.

For a Special Thrill

♥♡Men, have you ever felt your partner's climax? Women, have you ever felt the spasms of your orgasm, or is there usually too much going on? That was true for me until one evening, when Ed had already climaxed but was still inside of me when I came. The feeling, for both of us, was intense. For the first time, we shared the internal spasms of my body during orgasm. This can work for you, too. Ladies, as you feel yourself ready to come, ask your partner to hold very still. Then clench your vaginal muscles and, if you like, touch yourself or ask your partner to touch you to push yourself over that edge. It's an amazing feeling and will probably bring him to climax, as well.

For Fun

♥♡Here's a variation on the "hold still" game. While making love, challenge both of you by saying, "I don't want you to come until I give you permission." Hopefully, your partner will take you up on the dare, and the game is on. Can you make him or her come despite your partner's best efforts not to? And what will be the "punishment" if your lover cannot hold off the orgasm?

187

Saturday Night #38

A Most Intimate Kiss

Tonight's ideas revolve around oral sex. If this idea doesn't pique your interest, then turn to next week's suggestion. But remember, what doesn't intrigue you today might be of interest later on, and it might intrigue your partner, so you might just want to read on anyway.

I know there are many couples like Ed and me who really enjoy oral sex, both giving and receiving. If you are old hands at it, you might find some intriguing new temptations tonight. Unfortunately, the question of oral sex also causes one of the most common disagreements between husbands and wives. Frequently, one person wants to indulge, while the other doesn't. If your partner truly doesn't, it's time to adjust to that fact and add other delightful activities to your repertoire. But if you've always wanted to try performing oral sex on your partner or if you think you might be able to entice your partner into giving it a try, you'll especially enjoy tonight.

Please be very careful. If your partner's reluctant, the most important word is *entice*. Never force your partner to do anything. *Never.* In addition to the obvious, if you insist, either physically or emotionally, your partner might go along just to make you happy or to get it over with. However, a bad sexual experience makes it that much more difficult to initiate another encounter. Your partner, having been made unhappy, will put off your next meeting for as long as possible, not the outcome you had in mind at all.

You might be able to tempt your partner into putting his or her mouth on you. I'll get to how in a moment. First, let's investigate the why. Why won't he or she "go down on you"? Actually, the reasons are usually quite straightforward. First, many people have been brought up to believe that "nice girls or guys don't do that awful thing." Parents who themselves never learned to enjoy oral sex pass that feeling on to their children either overtly or subtly. How sad—to dislike something you've never tried. I was almost six years old before I tried chocolate pudding, because I didn't like what it looked like. I wouldn't be convinced. Of course, I eventually tried it and loved it. Lesson learned.

Second, a large number of folks, both men and women, are afraid of smelling or tasting something unpleasant. There are ugly jokes about how disgusting oral sex is and that keeps many people from trying. I've also gotten letters from women who've been forced to put their mouths on men and, from then on, vowed that they would never do it again, even for men they loved.

There's also a pervasive myth that I bought into for many years. Many people are sure there's some magic way to "do it right" and they are sure they don't know what that is. He thinks, She'll know I've never done it before, or she thinks, I've got to deep-throat and I know I'll gag. We'll talk about all of these reactions tonight.

How to entice? A few suggestions. First, be sure you're clean and be sure that your partner knows that. How? Easy. Suggest that you take a shower or bath together and then, once well washed, use your soapy hands to get your partner in the mood. Or splash in the hot tub, and then sit on the edge and suggest. Stroke, tease, and, in all the other ways you know, raise the heat level. Then ask gently if your lover will just lick once. Don't insist; just suggest. I've gotten several letters from people who've tried this approach and it's worked. Remember, the more excited you get your partner before the suggestion, the more likely he or she will be to give it a try. Just one lick, no more.

Of course, there's always chocolate sauce or maple syrup. It's a silly game and much teased about on TV, but it really does work. Choose something that has a strong smell and is really sticky, protect the sheets, and then play. Rub it on each other's nonthreatening areas first, licking it off as you go. Move on toward the genitals only after lots of laughter and excitement. Then, when you think the moment might be right, smear on quite a bit and suggest a sort of treasure hunt. Just for a moment. And keep your hands away from your partner while he or she indulges.

I got a letter recently from a woman whose ex-boyfriend used to hold her head pressed against his groin until she had satisfied him. We all know why he's her ex, of course. She said that she used to enjoy the activity but that now she was really afraid to use her mouth to pleasure her new lover because she was terrified of having her head held. She knew he would never do anything like that, but the fear ran deep. I suggested that she tie his hands loosely to the headboard of the bed to make herself more comfortable, and I got a truly grateful letter in return. It had worked for her, and it might work for you.

Whatever means you use to suggest oral sex, be sure your discussion is for only one or two licks, not a long oral-sex encounter. Move slowly. It's that first moment that's the most difficult.

How to do it? That's a really easy question to answer. Do what makes your partner, and you, of course, feel good. Each body is different and therefore what feels good is different for everyone. There are a few general things that should please. Lick gently, taking careful note of your partner's reaction. Do more of what makes him moan, less of what makes her pull back. Ask your partner to help you by loudly sighing and gently guiding your mouth to the parts that feel particularly good. And I do mean guiding, not pushing or pressing. Lick genitals with the flat of your tongue, then investigate crevices with the tip. Suck gently whenever the mood strikes you and keep your teeth covered at all times with your lips. Use your hands to increase the heat.

As you get more excited, add sensations. Put some cool wine in your mouth or hold an ice cube in your mouth. Use your rough tongue or suck more firmly, but whatever you do, use your partner's reactions as the best guide.

Partners, help your lover understand what you like and what you don't. Be really noisy. Say something. Use direct words: "That feels so good" or "Just like that, baby." Remember, it's really scary to perform oral sex for the first time, even if it's just the first time with a new partner, so be as gentle and helpful as you can be.

As for specific techniques? Here are a few suggestions.

For Her

❤ It's called fellatio. It can be really frightening the first time, but there are teases and tips that any woman can learn. Begin with a kiss. Just a kiss. While you're stroking him, place a kiss on his belly, one on his thigh, and one on his penis. That's wasn't too bad, was it? That's the way to begin. You've just taken the biggest step.

191

Okay, you've kissed. Now try a lick, like an all-day sucker. Pretend he's a Tootsie Pop. Explore and stop when you don't like it anymore. You can start and stop several times if you like. There's no pressure. Do you want to give him more pleasure?

For most men, the most sensitive areas of the penis are the tip, the rim and upper side of the head, and the lower, nonbelly side of the shaft. Form your lips in a tight O, use lots of saliva to make everything very slippery, and suck the tip into your mouth; then draw back so it pulls out. Just the first inch or so. You can also swirl your tongue over the head of his penis. Some men like to have the hole at the end teased, but for others, that's too sensitive to be pleasurable. Give it a try and see how he reacts.

Wrap your hand around the shaft while you play and slowly slide your hand toward the base. Play with his testicles lightly, and softly touch the perineum, the area between his testicles and his anus. If he enjoys this, do more, with firmer touches. Keep your hand wrapped around the shaft, which not only feels good for him but keeps his penis from penetrating too deeply into your mouth. If you pull the skin tightly downward, it can increase the intensity of the sensation for him.

Once you get a bit more comfortable with a small amount of penetration, try letting the shaft get sucked more deeply into your mouth. Now, pull your head back, maintaining the light suction as the penis withdraws. To add more stimulation, use the flat of your tongue along the lower side as you move. Move slowly or quickly, depending on how loudly he's moaning. If your mouth gets tired, the sucking part isn't important anymore; it's the sliding action of your lips and covered teeth. You don't have to force his penis so deeply into your mouth that it causes you to gag. Linda Lovelace has discouraged more women from trying oral sex than anyone else, by far. Whatever gives him pleasure is enough.

If your partner doesn't stay fully erect, that's normal. Sexual tension ebbs and flows. To keep him erect longer, use your thumb and index finger to form an O around the base of the shaft, creating a tight ring. This acts to restrict blood flow, keeping the penis stiff.

If you want to wander, kiss and lick his testicles. For many men, this is even better than having the penis played with. Don't suck too hard, however, as it can be quite painful.

About ejaculation. Men, until you're sure your partner is anxious to have a mouthful of your semen, don't ejaculate in her mouth. For some women, it is a wonderful experience to have a man come in their mouths, the ultimate compliment on their oral-sex skills. For a few women, it can be traumatic. For others, just icky. So discuss it with your partner. If you've agreed that, for the moment, you won't climax, don't let it happen. Have a signal between you that says, I'm going to come very soon. It can be as simple as saying just that. Remember, if you make it unpleasant, it will be a long time before she attempts it again.

For Him

It's called cunnilingus. Learning what pleases a woman can be a treasure, and there are as many techniques as for fellatio. You know what you want, but do you know what she wants? Here are a few techniques for you.

An important preliminary is to tell her you think she's beautiful and/or sexy. Don't be a phony, but tell her that she's sexy and hot and that her body excites you. Most women are very worried about their looks and their sex appeal. Don't overlook helping her feel good about herself.

Have you ever taken a good look at a woman's genitals? Well, do so. Get to know the landmarks—the outer lips, the inner ones, and, most important, her clitoris. Moisten a finger and explore. If you've just begun, don't touch the clitoris yet. Take your time. Before a woman's excited, and that can take awhile, she might not like to have her clitoris touched. There's no real technique to these explorations; just do what you think she's enjoying. Use some lubricant if she's not wet yet, and go slowly. I'm told that men don't particularly like to be teased. Women do. Nibble the insides of her thighs. Kiss. Lick. Slide your tongue along the crease where her thigh meets her pubic area. Use you fingers and your mouth.

Now explore all the creases with your tongue. Kiss the area. Tease lightly and then pull back. Hopefully, she'll be arching her back, trying to press her flesh to yours. Gently spread her legs with your hands, but don't hold her tightly. For a while, continue to avoid her clitoris, even though you know that's where she wants to be touched now. Try pushing the tip of your tongue deeply between the inner lips, as if you're penetrating her with it. But keep it gentle.

If her clitoris is now exposed, lick it gently. Feel for it with your tongue if you can't see it. If it's not hard, like a small pea beneath the surface, move away and play some more. Once it's swollen, part the lips, if necessary, and flick your tongue over it. It can be particularly erotic for you to hold her lips apart with your fingers while you lick. Please take care not to trap small hairs beneath your fingers. I can attest to the fact that it can really hurt.

Make a small O with your lips and suck on her clitoris. If she likes this, do more. For some women, however, this sensation is just too intense, so let her guide you. Most men stop too soon. If she's bucking with terrific pleasure, hang on and don't stop. You can bring her to climax just that way, and she'll love you for it.

Don't forget to use your hands while you're using your mouth. Slip one or two fingers inside of her and simulate intercourse. The in-and-out motion is sensational. If she likes it, play with her nipples. Many women, as they approach orgasm, like it a bit rough. Try lightly pinching one nipple and see whether it gives her pleasure.

Once she's climaxed, don't stop unless she makes it clear that she wants you to. Continued clitoral and vaginal stimulation can lead to multiple orgasms for many women. This might be the moment for intercourse, hard and fast, since she's already as hot as she can get.

One more thing. I'm not a big fan of sixty-nine, lying so that each can perform oral sex on the other. I like to do only one at a time. If I'm performing oral sex, I can't get much enjoyment out of receiving. You might want to alternate, but that's really up to you both.

For Fun

❤️ As you're about to indulge in the pleasures of oral sex, rinse your mouth with a minty mouthwash. It's quite a sensation.

For Fun

❤️ Try humming as you use your mouth. The vibrations will be transmitted to his or her genitals and create a fantastic buzz.

For Him

❤️ If she's reluctant because she's not sure how to do it, ask her to put one or two fingers in your mouth and demonstrate what you enjoy. If she's willing, ask her to do to your penis what you are doing to her finger.

Remember, good oral sex, like any other form of sex, isn't something you can learn overnight. It takes days, weeks, months, or even years of experimentation to discover what you each like. And it's the exploration and experimentation that are the pleasure. Practice makes perfect, you know, so practice a lot, but don't ever worry about being perfect.

195

Saturday Night #39

Water, Water

We think of water as a useful tool and a refreshing drink, but a sex toy? Absolutely.

For Him

♥♡Here's a wonderful way to spend an evening, as a prelude to something more or as a sensual activity by itself. While she's putting the kids to bed or finishing the dishes, run her a warm bath, filled with bubbles. If you don't have bubble bath, buy some or, if price is a problem, use a few drops of mild liquid dish-washing detergent. Fill the tub as high as it will go before reach-ing the overflow hole. You might even want to put duct tape over

the overflow opening so that you can fill the tub even higher. For a woman, getting both her breasts and her knees beneath the water at the same time can be an amazing luxury. Some water may slop on the floor, but that can be mopped up later.

If you're feeling so inclined, light several unscented candles and turn off the overhead light to increase the mood. I suggest unscented because I wouldn't add another odor to whatever suds are in the tub. Leave the scented candles or incense for another time. Just let the fragrance of the bubble bath fill the room. You might use a small radio, tuned to a favorite easy-listening station, or a favorite tape or CD to fill the room with soft music. Take care not to put any electrical appliance anywhere near the water, of course.

When all is prepared, invite your lady into the bathroom and slowly remove her clothes. Don't let her do it, and don't get too sexual. This is only the beginning. Help her into the water and guide her into a lounging position in the tub. Place a rolled towel behind her neck and have her rest her head and close her eyes. Then begin to soap one of her hands. Slowly, wash each finger, stroking it as if it were the most precious thing you've ever felt. You'll feel a bit strange at the start, but once you get into it, you'll discover the true sensuality of her slippery skin.

Continue with her arm and shoulder; then repeat the process with her other hand. Watch her face so you can share her sensual pleasure in what you're doing. You can also read whether what you're doing might be irritating. If so, just move on to another area.

Feet are tricky because many of us, myself included, are ticklish. But take the time to try the same slow washing, beginning at her toes. If she giggles, so what? We're exploring intimacy, not necessarily seduction, right now. You might find that sliding your little finger between her toes, pushing first one way, and then the other in that spot where almost no one's ever touched

197

her before, is really sexy. Of course, if she's not getting pleasure from your ministrations because she's ticklish, move on.

Continue with her leg only up to the knee; then massage her other foot and leg. By now, you've used lots of soap and the bubbles have probably begun to disappear. If the water's gotten cool, carefully add some hot so that the water's back up to bath temperature. Swish your hand around to make suds. If you happen to brush against some erogenous zone, so be it. But remember, don't be in a hurry.

Since you haven't touched any of her torso yet, it's now time to decide how to proceed. If you want to adjourn to the bedroom and make love there, let her soak for a few more moments and then have her stand up. If she wants, she can shower off before getting out, in order to remove the soap, but that might spoil the mood. You two decide. Either way, don't let her dry off herself. You use the towel and softly rub her all over. Find the thinnest towel you have, one that's been washed so many times you can feel her body through it. I know that fluffy is usually recommended, but I really prefer several small, thin kitchen towels so that you, and she, can feel everything. Something that Ed and I tease at is licking water from each other's bodies. That enticing drop that hangs from her nipple is a good place to start. If you want to play in the bathroom, you might lick the droplets from her mound, as well. You want her to be completely dry, don't you? Actually, she'll be wetter than usual. How delightful.

If you want to continue to play in the tub, then use your hands or a soapy facecloth to wash her breasts, playing special attention to her nipples. Blow some cool air over her hot, wet skin. Take your time. As you're expanding your soaping, take care not to get any in the vaginal canal. That can cause itching and irritation.

Where to go from here is strictly up to you, but now that you've set the mood, proceed slowly and savor each moment.

For Her

♥♡ How about surprising him in the shower? First, be sure you have plenty of time to play. This isn't something you want to rush. While he's showering, take off all your clothes and climb in behind him. Quickly rub soap all over your chest and massage his back with your wet, soapy body. Reach around from behind and wash his chest, his thighs, and, eventually, his genitals. Remaining behind him, rub your slick, slippery hands all over his erection. If he can't control himself, so much the better. This one's for his pleasure.

If you get this far, turn him around and rub his chest with yours, sliding your hands all over him, as though his body is the sexiest thing you've ever touched. It is, you know, and if you concentrate on that thought, you'll communicate that to him. If you're so inclined, get down on your knees and take him into your mouth. Don't worry about "doing it right"; just do it. There's no right or wrong way. Just the act of putting your mouth on him may drive him crazy. If you've always been reluctant to perform oral sex, here's just the place to start.

A few tips on mouths and penises and showers. Think of it as using your tongue to dry him off. Lap the water off his penis. Use your hands on his buttocks to brace yourself and stroke him as though he's covered with something delicious and you want to get every bit. It will give him tremendous pleasure, and if you have your radar well tuned, you can share his joy, as well. Use that radar to concentrate on the things that make his knees shake and his thigh muscles clench. Maybe he'll want to continue in the bedroom, maybe he'll make passionate love to you right there, or maybe, if you're lucky, he won't be able to control himself and he'll just let it happen.

Don't worry if some semen gets on you. You're in the shower, after all. If some gets into your mouth, don't panic. It's not bad-tasting, just thick, gooey, and slightly tangy. If it offends, open your mouth and rinse, very quietly. But be complimented. He's just told you that he's so excited by your ministrations that he can no longer control his body. What a wonderful thing you've just done. Bravo!

For Fun

♥♡ Making love in a hot tub always seemed like a great idea to me, until I tried it. Actually, my partner found that his spirit was willing, but his penis just wouldn't stay erect. Such is the problem with some men and hot (or very cold) water. So if you want to fool around, give yourselves some time to get adjusted.

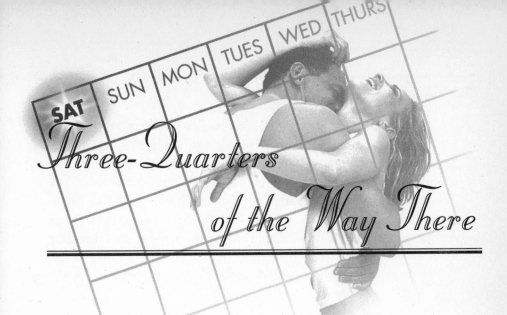

Three-Quarters of the Way There

Okay, by now you've found a few new things that you really enjoy, and that's great. You also run the risk, however, of settling on a few activities and not trying anything new.

So now, in the last quarter of this book, let's get more adventurous. Some of the activities are a bit off the beaten path, so if you begin to read and find a section isn't to your taste, skip it. But keep an open mind. It's amazing that as your horizons broaden, you begin to think of erotic pleasures in ways you never did before.

Will he think you're kinky for considering something really unusual? Not if you mention it lightly, with all the options open. Wouldn't it be a shame if you both wanted the same thing and neither of you ever mentioned it? How much pleasure will be bypassed?

So be brave and suggest a tiny step in a different direction.

If your partner mentions something you feel is not a great idea, remember that he or she has taken a risk by asking, so tread gently. Remember that even though it may be a less-than-wonderful idea, your partner is wonderful for taking the risk of mentioning it. That shows a lot of love and trust. So here's your big opportunity. If your partner's idea isn't to your taste, mention something else that you've always wanted. Even if it takes a few bounces, something new and creative will evolve. Count on it!

Saturday Night #40

Betcha

*A*re there things you want in bed that you've never had the courage to ask for? I'll bet there are. We are all timid at times, thinking that our desires are the oddest in the world and that if our partner ever found out that we wanted to make love on the coffee table, or tied to the bed, he or she would be horrified. That's probably not the case at all.

Here's a way to wander into new areas of sexuality.

Tonight, play a game for forfeits. I don't care what game, just so there's a winner and a loser. The winner gets to control the sexual events for, say, one hour. He or she gets to ask for whatever is desired, from a hair brushing to oral sex. Remember, it's not a demand and this isn't done to *force* anyone to do anything repugnant, but it can guide you into new realms.

How might this play out?

203

Let's say that you and your partner sit down for an evening of gin rummy. You play for a while, accumulating points, when you lightly suggest that the loser of the next hand will have to put the dinner dishes away or the winner gets to decide on the TV show after the game. Okay, you two agree. That's not too difficult. Later on, you make another bet, similar to the first one. You're on your way.

It's getting late and you're feeling daring. You suggest that the loser of the next game owes the winner half an hour of servitude. For now, it doesn't have to be sexual. Let's work into that gradually. You can suggest a back rub, or a late-night snack in bed—whatever seems delicious at the time.

On another night, you finally play a game for the ultimate prize, a half an hour of *sexual* servitude. It can get silly if you want it to, thus taking some of the pressure off. But think about the opportunities you now have if you're the winner or even the loser. They are both of value.

If you're the winner, you can ask for what you want. Start slowly if you don't want to take big risks, but be brave. Take a bit of the initiative and request something new.

♡   I want half an hour of really sexy kissing.
♡   I want fifteen minutes of slow dancing; then I'll decide what's next.
♡   Darling, run me a bubble bath and then strip.

Whatever you've always wanted. Go further? Sure, why not.

♡   Darling, I want you to play with me with your hands. I'll tell you where and how to touch me, but you have to touch where and how I say for my half an hour.
♡   Strip and wait for me on the living room carpet.
♡   I want you to wake me in the morning with your mouth.

You can, and should, ask for whatever you want. Realize that this a dialogue designed to give you the freedom to ask for new and exciting activities.

If you're the loser, there's just as much opportunity to explore. Now you're going to learn what your partner wants in terms of sex. Go along and be careful so as not to seem judgmental. Flow with it, and you will probably find that you'll have an evening to remember. Realize that your partner is taking a considerable risk and that you can either encourage new and delicious activities in the bedroom or squash your partner's creativity for what might be the last time.

It's possible that something he or she suggests may be repugnant to you. Okay, find something related that you think you can deal with and suggest a slightly different path. For example, if he wants you to perform oral sex on him and you really can't, then suggest that you can stroke him instead. Or that you'll lick the end but that you can't put his penis into your mouth. Just don't condemn.

Always pay careful attention and store away your lover's desires for the next time you make love. If she asks to tie you up, maybe you can get her a length of rope for a gag gift. If she wants to be blindfolded, buy a beautiful scarf that can double as a blindfold.

If the evening turns out well, and if you both relax and give a bit, it will, then try it again during the week. Maybe the loser will be the winner next time. Maybe you can suggest something even more daring, like watching your partner masturbate or giving or receiving a mild spanking. A little creativity and a splash of daring will reap generous rewards.

Saturday Night # 41

Watch the Birdie

Tonight's fun and games are for couples with a bit of adventure in their soul. You and your partner have been venturing further and further into the realm of creative sex, so tonight, let's take another step. This evening you're going to take photos.

You'll need a Polaroid or a video camera. Why not a regular camera? Believe me, you won't want to take this type of photo to the local one-hour developing place. It's much better to have pictures that don't need processing.

Don't think that you have to look like a *Playboy* or *Playgirl* centerfold to be the subject of an erotic photo. These are for the two of you and only for the two of you. They will be stimulating both because they will be erotic and because they will bring back memories of a night of great sex, because that is exactly what will happen.

Where to start? First, relax and get mellow. This can be one of the sexiest evenings you've had in a long time, but it's difficult to begin. So have a glass of wine or a few beers and nurture sexy feelings. Next, decide who's going to go first. One of you will take the photos and one will be the model. The photographer will be the one more in charge, playing director as much as he or she likes. The one being photographed needs to have courage, for this will be awkward at first.

Okay, now play for a while. Get warmed up. Then, when you're ready, have the camera handy.

To start with, take some glamour shots. The model should get all dolled up, with carefully combed hair and such. Have some photos taken fully clothed, looking really sexy. Pose with a "come hither" glance, a suggestive angle of your knee, a knowing look in your eye. Not only will this give your partner something for his or her wallet; it will get you comfortable with the camera.

Do the same thing with your video camera. Pretend you're in a PG-rated movie and can't do anything too overt. Just suggest with your body and your voice. Say sexy, teasing things; beckon with a curl of your finger. Urge the camera and your lover to get closer. Remember how Marilyn Monroe made love to the camera? Picture Rudolph Valentino in those old silent films. I know you can do it.

Let's say that he's the photographer and she's the model, and let's begin with a Polaroid. Take a few photos of her face, her hands, parts of her that aren't overtly erotic. You'll be surprised later on to see that her face, flushed and excited, and her hands, ready to touch and caress, are really just as erotic as her most intimate parts. Now she can begin to undress, if she hasn't already done so. Take lots of pictures of her partially clothed, revealing a shoulder or a breast. Have extra film handy so you can snap away. Many of the pictures will be terrible, but you can just chuck them and keep the ones that arouse. When she is finally nude, include shots of her hands touching her breasts or mound. He can also direct the action. "Move a bit this way. . . . Touch your nipple so I can get a better shot." I know it sounds a bit clinical, but it's not. Believe me!

207

If you have a video camera, even better. Ed bought a small hand-held camera a few years ago and we used it together for vacations and pictures of my grandchildren. Good uses, but in the back of both of our minds were other things we could photograph. But neither of us mentioned it for months. Eventually, we talked about it and discovered that we were both excited and totally daunted by the idea. Occasionally, one of us would say, "You know, we really have to take dirty pictures of each other one night." And the other would say, "Right, we really do."

It didn't happen until one evening we got a bit blitzed, then got very excited by the idea. Finally, Ed just took out the camera and spent a long time connecting it to the TV. He wanted to be able to take the movies and watch them on the screen at the same time. He fiddled for fifteen minutes while I cooled off. By the time everything was connected, I wasn't sure I wanted to do it. How would I look? I'm not young anymore and I sag in lots of places I'd rather I didn't.

Ready? he asked when he finally had the wires working.

I sighed, knowing that Ed loves me just the way I am. In for a penny, I thought. He tried to prop the camera on the dresser and shoot toward the bed, but found that it was really difficult to stay in the frame. I know it can be done, even without a tripod, but that night it just wasn't working. So he held the camera and aimed it at me.

Somehow I didn't want my face in the pictures, at least not yet, so I said, "Aim it at the center of the bed." I moved so my body was center-frame and opened my shirt, looking everywhere but at the TV, on which the shots were being shown. I didn't want to see anything just yet. I won't go into every detail, but as time passed I got more comfortable and finally glanced at the TV. I gasped. Was that erotic image me? He was shooting between my spread legs and my fingers were clearly visible in the picture. I was a center-fold. I loved it. As I watched, I began to perform for the camera, moving so Ed could get better angles. It was wonderful.

As Ed continued to shoot, I became a bit impatient for him and

finally told him, "Put that camera down and get over here." The rest, as they say, is history. It was explosive. We still have the tape, but I haven't seen it. For me, the photographic session was the fun. Maybe eventually we'll watch it. Maybe Ed does when I'm not around in the flesh.

Occasionally since then, we've gotten out the camera and one or the other of us has taken pictures. It's not a frequent thing for us, but on the occasional evening, it's dynamic.

For Fun

❤ For couples who have to be separated for a Saturday night or two, take some erotic pictures of yourself and send one to your partner while he or she is away. How? First, you need a camera that either has a control to delay the photo for thirty seconds so you can position yourself or that has a remote so you can snap and be in the picture at the same time. Then pose and snap away. Once you have a particularly naughty photo, mail it to your partner. Or, better still, if you have a digital camera that can interface with your computer, or a scanner, E-mail the photo or post it on a private Web page for only your lover to see.

If you have a video camera, it can be easier to get pictures. Find a spot where you can prop the camera so that it has a good view of the bed, or a chair. Then push the record button and indulge. Play. Perform. Be really daring. And don't look at the movie or you'll chicken out. Just send it to him.

For Fun

❤ I gather that there are hookups that you can get that enable two people to video-talk over the Internet. See the possibilities? *209*

Saturday Night #42

Money Can Be the Root of Fantastic Sex

There are several ways to use money as a sex toy. Here are just two suggestions for tonight.

<u>PAY FOR SEX?</u>

Maybe . . . if the person you're paying is your partner. What happens when you pay for sex? You can ask for anything you want. So here's a delicious way to spend an evening.

For Her

❤♡ Hire a gigolo—your partner. Pay him in either real or play money for an hour of exclusive sex. You can ask for an erotic massage, or have him touch you just where you want. But whatever you do, you must ask specifically for what you want. He is a "stranger" who doesn't know you at all, so you have to take the initiative. Do you want a missionary-position quickie? I don't think that's the way you would choose to spend your money. If you've got him, use him.

For Him

❤♡ Be that gigolo she's hired. Please her, but urge her to ask for what she wants. That accomplishes two different things. First, it helps you to understand what she likes in bed—or on the dining room table. Make careful mental notes of what she desires. Is it hard and fast or slow and tempting? Does she like intercourse, or does she prefer being touched and brought to climax with your hands? Where does she want your mouth, your fingers?

There's a second benefit from making her ask for what she wants. It's incredibly erotic to say the words, to be bold enough to suggest something different. But she can do it, since she's paid for your services.

STRIP FOR MONEY

For Her

❤♡ Become a paid stripper. Suggest that your husband have lots of money, real or Monopoly, handy, because he'll find good ways to spend it later. Now dress for the part. Find your sexiest undies, *211* or take some old ones and cut holes in strategic places—holes that allow your nipples to show, or let him see a tuft of pubic hair. Have you got a garter belt and stockings, or maybe some old garters? Take care if you want to use rubber bands to hold up your hose, since they can cut off circulation and do damage. But really big, loose ones work just fine and can hold up the legs cut from an old pair of panty hose if you haven't any stockings. Stockings are a must for stripping. It's such a thrill for both of you and your partner to watch as you peel down your stockings really slowly.

If you have some old cotton or, better still, satin gloves, wear those so you can remove them very slowly and tease him with them.

Wear clothes that are tight and revealing, but not difficult to remove. If you struggle to take off a pair of tight pants, it might spoil the mood. Or maybe not. Maybe you can ask him to help. If you've nothing suitable, take some of those clothes that were destined for the Salvation Army and cut them up. Shorten the skirt, lower the neckline, get rid of the sleeves.

If you're a bit intimidated, there are lots of movies with strip scenes in them, everything from Demi Moore in *Striptease* and Natalie Wood in *Gypsy,* to self-help films, to X-rated flicks. Watch what the women in the film do and make mental notes. Remember, this is all a tease, a game. Have confidence. You know you can do it, and, wow, the rewards will be amazing.

Select some sexy music with lots of brass and a hard beat. Then practice grinding your hips in front of the mirror. Will you feel silly? Yup. Take the plunge anyway. Do it.

For Him

❤You're now the customer with wads of money. Stuff it down the front of her blouse, into the waistband of her panties.

Reward her with deep, long looks or hoots of delight. Encourage her, because you can imagine how embarrassing it is. But it's also fun for you both.

Yell, "Take it off," and "Come on, baby, strut your stuff." Whistle. In general, be an appreciative yet a bit disruptive audience. The more you encourage, the braver she'll become, and you'll reap the benefits. "Ten bucks for your panties. Okay, make it a hundred." You've got money to burn, and she's all yours.

LET'S TURN THE TABLES

For Him

♥♡ Did you see the film *The Full Monty*? In that movie, several men want to make some money by becoming male strippers. Well, why should women have all the fun? For another night, become a male stripper like the Chippendale guys. What to wear? A tight pair of jeans and a tight T-shirt will do just fine. Wear a belt that you can slowly pull from its loops and maybe a pair of leather gloves that you can remove and toss to your audience. Forget wearing socks, since I think they are difficult to remove erotically. If you can find a tight G-string or pouch, wear one beneath your jeans as a special surprise for your partner.

How to strip? The way a man strips isn't very different from the way a woman does. Put on some music with a strong beat, then strut, emphasizing your assets: your bare chest, your tight ass, your genitals. Bump and grind. Tease by getting close, then moving away. Wiggle so your buttocks or crotch gets really close to her face. If you really want to play, oil your chest, thighs, and arms before stripping.

Does it feel silly? Yes . . . but not for long.

For Her

❤♡While he's warming up, be encouraging. Scream, "Take it all off!" and "Let's see your gorgeous body!" Get into it. Stuff money down the front of his shorts. Grab at his groin as he teases, but don't necessarily touch him yet or, if you do, just a quick tweak. Make it all last.

Remember that it's all a game. Play it!

Saturday Night #43

Sex and the Internet— Hot Chatting

I'm sure you've heard about Internet chat rooms. They are places in cyberspace where people who share common interests can gather and talk. The interests can be as varied as fly-fishing and astrology, *Star Trek* and living in Washington, D.C., cooking vegetarian meals and photography. You just go to a chat room, watch what others are talking about, and join in when you wish. That talk can get as hot as you like, in rooms devoted to every sexual topic imaginable.

You can, of course, hot-chat by yourself anytime you want, but, for tonight, after the kids are in bed and the phone has stopped ringing, it's time for you and your partner to fire up the computer and get down and dirty on-line. As you'll see, you can make it clear to your on-line counterpart that you are a couple or you can take on a single identity and play that way. If one of you has already logged on and has seen what goes on, that's great.

You or your lover can be the expert. If neither of you have ever tried it, here's an opportunity to play a new game together.

How do you start hot-chatting? I'm an AOLer, so I can best discuss AOL's chat rooms, but IRC chats, ones for those using other Internet service providers, run pretty much the same way. On AOL, you click to go to chat rooms in general, then click to go to a special section called Member Chats. There you'll find dozens of rooms listed in which people are discussing sexual topics, from corporal punishment to lesbian relationships, from where to find strip clubs in Seattle to "lonely wife needs company."

What do the titles mean? The room names are merely a way for you to select your specific area of interest, or curiosity. Once you click on a room, you'll find yourself in an "area" in which folks are exchanging typed messages on whatever topic you selected. Actually, the conversation might have shifted from the main topic to something quite different. You just have to read along and see what's going on. Be aware that there will probably be several discussions going on at a time, so you might have to spend a few minutes adjusting to reading every third or fourth line to follow one thread. Once your brain adjusts, you'll be able to enjoy listening in on an interchange between two, or even among more people. You're not eavesdropping, by the way. All the people chatting are completely aware that others are "lurking."

At some point, you might receive a private note (called an "Instant Message" in AOLspeak) from someone wanting to know who you are and whether you're interested in a private chat. Now's the time to take a moment and decide who you are. Are you just yourself? Sure, if that's what you like, but remember, you don't have to be you. You can assume a persona the way you would put on a suit of clothes. No one knows who you are or anything about you. They know your screen name and nothing more. Do you want to be older? Younger? Another race or religion? Do you want to be from another part of the country? Do you want to change your sex and be a man (or woman) for a while? It's all possible.

That makes it imperative for you to accept that the people on the other side of the screen can do exactly the same thing. Does it matter to you whether he or she is really five feet tall or Asian? Not a whit. They are who they want to be for the night, and you are whoever you want to be. Maybe you and your partner enter a chat room to read and type together, pretending to be a twenty-two-year-old female. Go for it. Anything's possible.

Answer the instant message or don't—that's up to you. But relax and go along with what's happening. It might be embarrassing, but who cares? You're in private, by yourself or with just your partner. You can giggle, blush, whatever. No one can see you.

Slowly, you'll adjust to what's going on in the chat room. You'll be able to follow conversations and get comfortable with the topic under discussion. If you're not, just click to another room.

Eventually, you'll probably want to jump in and type a question, or a response. Just let your fingers go with your mind. If you can't type, that's no problem. Use two fingers, hunt and peck, and soon you'll be typing quickly enough to keep up.

At first, you'll probably feel really silly, and if you are uncomfortable with four-letter words, you might find it difficult to see them spelled out on the screen. When I first logged on, I was amazed and a bit shocked to see what went on. It took only a short time, however, for me to get into the swing of it all, and you will, too. Just remember not to take it too seriously. It's all fun and games.

You might, at some point, be invited into a private room. On AOL, it's pretty simple. You and the one who invites you agree on a room title, click on "Private Room," and then type in the room name you've decided upon. Presto, you're there, just the two of you, together, sort of. No one else can see what you two are typing, so you can get as explicit as you like.

217

If you're enjoying yourself, terrific. Get into dirty typing. Play Truth or Dare, a game common in chat rooms. Do you have to tell the truth? Of course not. Be creative when asked what's the most unusual place you've ever had sex. Do you have to do what you've been dared to do? Certainly not. But if you want to take off your shirt, do it. It can be a lot of fun, and very exciting.

The rooms come and go and not all rooms are open at all times. Frequently, there are chat rooms for couples, where both partners are watching the screen and responding to questions and comments. Ed and I tried that a while ago, with mixed results. We chatted with one couple (at least we were told it was a couple) and we adjourned to a private room. We suggested various activities back and forth and had a rousing time. At another time, however, we got involved and the other folks just disappeared, and at another, it deteriorated into the other couple and me, leaving Ed out. They wanted a threesome, and poor Ed felt like the odd man out.

So enter rooms, see what's going on and leave, lurk, or join in. Stay or, if you want, click and move on. It's completely up to you and your tastes.

A few basic rules for hot-chatting. Never give out *any* personal information about yourself, such as your full name and city, or your phone number. Remember there are kooks out there. You wouldn't give out such information to someone you met five minutes before in a bar, so don't here, either. Even if he or she sounds like someone from heaven, don't. Remember that you can make up a persona and so can the person you're chatting with. If something makes you uncomfortable, log off. It's just as simple as hanging up on an obscene phone call.

I know that most of the people reading this book are partnered, but for those of you who might be tempted to enter relationships with folks you meet on-line, I feel it's important to warn you about

Internet romances. Here's what often happens. You meet on-line and chat. Things are great and you agree on times and chat rooms, and as more time passes, you feel more intimate. You discuss your life, your dreams, interests, jobs, political views, and outlook on life in every form imaginable. You might even have sex on-line, masturbating and exchanging messages at the same time. Maybe you graduate from chat rooms to a private room, and then to phone calls. You develop what feels like a serious, intimate relationship.

I get letters from people who are ready to move to wherever their Internet partner is and live happily ever after with someone they've "known" for many months. Please accept the fact that you really don't know each other at all. It's a false intimacy. You have always been on your best behavior with each other. You've never been exposed to him with a terrible head cold or her with a bad case of PMS. You haven't had to deal with his messy room or her constantly hanging wet nylons in the bathroom. You know only the good things and none of the bad habits.

Please be very cautious. If you want to meet, wonderful. But do it in a bailout situation, where either of you can call it off at any time. If you are in the same city, meet in a restaurant for dinner, without exchanging home addresses. Get to know each other up close before you do anything more. Take your own car so you can leave if you like. If you want to go further, do it in a safe location like a motel, not at your house or your partner's. Okay, I might seem a bit paranoid, but just be careful.

If you live in different cities and want to spend a weekend together, agree in advance that whoever's traveling will take a hotel room and you two will split the cost. That way, if it doesn't work out, you're not stuck in the same apartment together until the return flight.

Remember, you can always move to the more intimate, but it's really difficult to back off.

Hot-chatting can be a delicious activity for an evening for one person or a couple. Sign on and enjoy. Your mouse will never tell. *219*

Saturday Night #44

Mirror, Mirror, on the Ceiling

I think mirrors as a part of great sex have taken a bad rap. Sex and mirrors have been combined in some of the raunchiest stories, and in a way, that's too bad. Mirrors can be the most stimulating toys. You don't have to have one on the ceiling, although that's not a bad idea.

Have you ever watched yourself and your partner make love? I'll wager not. So let's try to find a way to do that this evening.

One way is to get suitably hot and bothered, then wander into the bathroom. There's that nice mirror over the sink. With one of you facing the mirror, the other can stand behind, reach around, and fondle breasts or his penis while both watch. It's an incredibly erotic sight, those deeper-toned hands on pale flesh. One of you can place hands over the other's while those hands roam. The recipient can take advantage of this position to guide those hands, so they touch all the best places.

Do you have a full-length mirror on the back of the closet door? Even better. That way, as one touches, both can watch the entire scene. Maybe his hands can wander downward while her eyes and hands follow every move. And guide them, too. You can exchange places and she can fondle your erect penis while you both watch.

If you find that enticing, take the next step. Prop a large mirror on your dresser so that you can watch yourself and your partner the next time you make love. I have one of those three-paneled mirrors on my dresser, so I can move into just the right position. The first time I watched as Ed and I made love, I was a bit shocked. I looked so hedonistic. But I will cheerfully admit that it was really exciting and that I do it often now.

If you've positioned the mirror, tell your partner about it. Softly, in the heat of passion, whisper, "Look at the mirror. See how we look when we make love. Watch my hands and yours. Look at us." It might be a shock, but a truly erotic one. Now perform as if you were a porn star. Show off those sexy body parts for the one who's now watching you. Touch your partner, or, even sexier, touch yourself. Watch your hands and your lover's as they join in giving pleasure. See how the fingers move. Wonderful, isn't it?

The large, convenient mirrored bathrooms are one of the sexiest things about some motel rooms. I've made love sitting sideways on the counter, with my partner and I watching every move. I can tell you from experience that it's really hard to tear your gaze away from hands and breasts and genitals. I ended up sitting on the counter with my legs over the edge, a very convenient height indeed.

In those hedonistic motels, mirrors are everywhere, including the ceiling. What a rush it is to watch.

If you want to think about mirroring the ceiling in your bedroom, here's a word of advice, though. Don't try to do it yourself. This is one area where hiring a professional contractor is most important. You don't want something to come crashing down onto the bed, with you and your partner in it. Don't worry about what the contractor will think. Will he think you two are kinky? Maybe. So what? He'll probably be envious. Let him drool!

Saturday Night #45

See No Evil—It's Much More Fun

*I*t's said that when we are deprived of one sense, our others become more acute. When we're blindfolded, for example, we can smell more subtle flowers, hear softer whispers, feel gentler caresses. And when used to enhance lovemaking, being blindfolded can be delightfully sinful. Let's give it a try tonight.

Making love with my eyes covered was one of the first slightly off-center erotic activities I indulged in. I found that when I made love with my eyes closed, as I usually do, I would open them occasionally and be jerked back into the real world. The lights in the bedroom were a bit harsher than in my completely sensual world. One Saturday night, I put a pillow lightly over my face, and it changed things, as it can for you tonight.

How will it feel? I can only tell you how it was for me. When Ed first covered my eyes, I drifted into another world. It wasn't really different from my bedroom, but the edges were softer, the way movie close-ups are sometimes when they are shot through a greased lens to make them slightly gauzy. I found that I felt lovemaking more acutely. I didn't know exactly what Ed was going to do next and I couldn't look to see. And Ed was, and still is, very inventive.

Here's how it might work for you.

For Either of You

❤♡ Suggest that you'd like to be blindfolded. "How about using that scarf and covering my eyes while we make love?" Your partner's probably going to wonder what to do once the blindfold is in place. Tell your lover to do what you two normally do, just do it a bit more slowly. Then help tie the blindfold tightly enough so you really cannot see.

I remember playing Pin the Tail on the Donkey as a kid. I was afraid of being really embarrassed by placing the donkey's tail on his nose, so I adjusted the blindfold so I could look down and see out just above my cheeks. Therefore, my tail always ended up in the right place. Maybe you did that, too.

In this case, that's not what we want to happen. If you can't get the blindfold on right, try this. Put a cotton ball over each closed eye and then tie on the blindfold. You won't be able to see then, and that's the fun of this.

Now let your mind wander. Think about how he looks or what she's going to do next.

♡ Will she touch my chest? Kiss my lips? Touch her breasts to my thighs?
♡ Will he rub his cheek over my belly? Lick my nipple? Bite a toe?
♡ Will she brush a feather across my lips?
♡ Will he scrape his nails over my hip?

223

How delicious to think about all these things, and how exciting. If your partner is blindfolded, a wonderful thing to do is to tell him or her, in great detail, what you're anticipating doing to his or her luscious body. Don't do it yet; discuss it first.

When it's time for intercourse, tell your lover what you're going to do and let him or her feel your movements on the bed.

For Both of You

♥♡ Erotic images are much easier to create when you're not bombarded by the real sights of your bedroom. So, while your lover is blindfolded, create the sights. Words have additional power when your partner can't see. It's all the easier to become part of a scene. Describe a scenario as different from your current one as you can think of.

♡ We're alone in a garden and it's late on a summer afternoon. It's really hot and your body's covered with a slick film of sweat. We're lying on a blanket and you can feel the hot sun beating down on your naked belly.

♡ We're in my office and it's very late. I've been working all day and you arrive to bring me dinner. We eat on my desk, then begin talking about our erotic evening last Saturday. Suddenly, I move all the dinner dishes off the desk and begin to undress you.

♡ It's snowing really hard and we're getting a bit nervous. We've been skiing and the trail's rapidly disappearing. We see a small hut usually used by the ski patrol for keeping equipment, but it looks warm and dry. We try the door and it's open. We leave our skis outside and find that there's a fireplace with a fire already laid. I light it and we take off our wet clothes. We can feel the warmth as the fire roars.

♡ You arrive at my office and I'm really busy. I have to take this phone call, but you're really hungry. You crawl under the desk and open your shirt. I know exactly what you're going to do.

For Fun

♥♡ Tell your blindfolded partner what you are going to do in great detail before you do it. Give him or her a few alternatives. "Maybe I'll kiss your lips or maybe I'll bite your nipple. Which do you think I should do?"

For Fun

♥♡ Touch or lick different parts of the body in rapid succession so that your lover doesn't know where your hands or lips will be next.

For Fun

♥♡ Hold a buzzing vibrator near your blindfolded partner's ear and discuss exactly what you are going to do with it.

You get the idea. Let your mind wander. Not very good at telling stories? It's not really difficult, so relax and give it a try.

Saturday Night #46

Loving Gestures

Life gets ordinary and commonplace. Take advantage of each day and be glad that you have a partner who's as wonderful as yours. Then let your lover know how you feel. There are several ways. Simple loving gestures can make your partner's toes tingle.

♡ Mention what a good lover your partner is. In public. It's embarrassing, but such a turn-on.

♡ So many folks have Web sites now, so if you do, here's a nice thing to do. Add a page that tells your lover how much you care. Add a picture if you have the ability, and make the whole thing really mushy.

♡ Did you used to have a ridiculous pet name for your partner? Use it. It's silly, but delightfully emotional.

♡ Tell your partner what sexy hands he or she has and how you can't wait to feel them on your skin.

♡ Find one of those photo booths and let the camera take a picture of the two of you soul-kissing. Or worse. Or better.

♡ Touch him or her as you walk past. A quick stroke on the back of the neck as you return to your table in a restaurant is particularly delicious. Hold hands.

♡ Rub your lover's palm erotically with your thumb, even when you think others might see. Especially when others might see.

♡ Have you got two phone lines in your house? Call him or her up from the next room and talk dirty. That way, you won't have to wait to act on a suggestion.

♡ Put a note on the refrigerator that says, "Make love tonight."

♡ Really kiss in public and make all around you envious.

Give your lover a present that's unusual and fun, whether for a real occasion or a silly anniversary like three years from the day you first kissed. Or take a sexy gift home for no reason at all. Here are a few ideas.

♡ A hairbrush to use on your lover's hair or for your partner to use on your buttocks.

♡ Edible undies or flavored condoms.

♡ Bubble bath, or a new, very different aftershave or perfume to help change your partner's image for the evening.

♡ A jar of thick jam, honey, or maple syrup.

♡ A ribbon to tie around your lover's wrist so that every time he or she looks down, there you'll be.

♡ A gift certificate at the local nail salon. Suggest that she get her nails done long and bright red so she can scratch them down your back.

♡ A magic wand so your partner can wave it and get any pleasure, large or small, desired. Or allow your lover to give it to you. Then use it!

♡ A roll of Saran Wrap to use as gift wrap. Or drape yourself in nothing but Christmas lights and interrupt your partner's TV watching.

♡ Dress in old clothes and gift wrap a pair of scissors so your lover can slowly cut off each garment, loving each part as it's revealed.

♡ A note with a genuine compliment, one that comes from the heart. For example: "I love the color of your eyes," or "The sight of your bare chest makes my knees weak."

♡ A stuffed animal that you can use later to caress your lover's body.

♡ A bunch of balloons on which you've written sexy words, such as *slippery, thighs, erotic, naked, wet*—you get the idea.

♡ A new set of sheets. Maybe satin? Or just a satin pillowcase.

♡ Gift wrap a cruise brochure and spend an evening creating an entire trip, including the stateroom with the DO NOT DIS-TURB sign on the door.

Prepare a surprise for your lover. How about doing something to change the atmosphere in the bedroom?

♡ Candlelight is so romantic. Add to the appeal by adding a drop of an aromatherapy oil to the top. Try apple, vanilla, or peach.

♡ Wear something different to bed. If you normally wear pajamas, climb between the sheets wearing nothing. If you always sleep bare, try a pair of briefs or a slip. How about a very tight T-shirt? Burn those old flannel pajamas, unless he likes to peel you open.

♡ Kiss good night with your eyes open.

♡ Substitute a softly colored bulb for the bright one in your lover's bedside lamp.

Sometimes the tiniest things can put a spark into your

relationship.

Saturday Night #47

Erotic Beginnings —Part 4

Here is a final group of fantasy story starters, these for the more adventurous. These tales can go in any direction you choose, so take your time and see where the adventures lead.

THE HAREM

"You saved my son's life," the sultan said.

"It was not a large thing, Your Highness," the knight responded, his eyes taking in the opulence of the sultan's clothing and the silver trappings on his horse. He stood quietly in front of a palace that rivaled anything he'd seen anywhere in the world, trying not to stare.

"It is to me, and it is to my son, whom you have restored to me. What is your name, sir?"

"Wilfred of East Essex, Your Highness."

"Those who are honored by me and by my court are allowed to call me Haran."

Wilfred bowed his head. He knew what an honor had just been accorded him. "Thank you, Your Highness—I mean, Haran."

"Sir Wilfred," Haran said, "you will be honored in my cottage tonight." He waved his arm at the magnificent dwelling. "There will be a feast, and you will receive your true reward."

His cottage, Wilfred thought. A palace with dozens of rooms, at least seven outbuildings, and gardens and grounds that would take weeks to explore and appreciate. He had really done very little. He had been wandering the land, seeing what there was to see before returning to his own country. Haran's son Benat had been wounded in battle and a fierce enemy warrior had held a sharpened sword to his throat. Wilfred had been attracted by the sounds of the battle, and although this wasn't his fight, he couldn't let anyone kill a helpless man, so he attacked and killed the enemy warrior. Not knowing who the now-unconscious young man was, he had carried the youth two miles to one of the healers' tents. It was only then that he discovered that the man he'd saved was the sultan's son. When the word had been passed to the sultan, Wilfred had been conducted to the palace.

Wilfred smiled, showing even white teeth. He would, of course, accept his reward. It wouldn't do to insult his host. He was led through the palace, bathed by four veiled but curvaceous young maidens, and given a magnificent scarlet-and-gold robe to wear.

The feast took several hours. He was served a dozen courses, the most exotic and delicious of foods from the far corners of the known world. There had been a hundred guests, but finally only he and the sultan remained, each reclining on thick cushions scattered over the many brightly colored carpets. "I will now withdraw," the sultan said, rising to his feet, "and you shall have the rest of your reward."

"I'm afraid I don't understand, Haran," Wilfred said. He had

already been given a jeweled dagger and a bolt of the finest silken cloth. As he walked from the otherwise-empty room, Haran merely smiled and clapped his hands. Then he disappeared through a curtained doorway.

From behind another curtain came three of the most exquisite women Wilfred had ever seen. Each was barefoot and had filmy gauze draped over her otherwise-unbound hair. Each woman was dressed in a tiny open jacket and matching full-legged pants. The first girl was blond, had fair skin, and was dressed in deep yellow-orange. "I am called Amber," she said, bowing. The second had long, flowing black hair, skin the color of smoke, and eyes that were almost black, and she wore the softest lavender. "I am Lilac." The third had skin the color of ebony and curly black hair, and she wore gauze of the softest ivory. "I am called Pearl."

"We are for you," they said in unison.

Wilfred gasped. Could they mean what they were saying? This wasn't the way of his land. Were these women slaves? Shouldn't he object?

Amber stepped forward. "It would be the deepest insult to reject us. Let us pleasure you."

This is a foreign country, he thought, and I really should abide by their ways. Wilfred settled back on his cushions. "I have been away from home for a long time and I have never seen anyone as beautiful as each of you." As the three women settled on pillows around him, he sipped wine from a golden goblet. "I'd be a fool to turn down such a generous offer."

THE PARTY

Why did I come? Elaine wondered as she dropped her coat on a chair at the side of the room. She'd stopped taking dares when she was twelve, and she knew what kind of a party this was going to be. Everyone knew that Stephanie's parties were nothing more than orgies. So why had she agreed to come? She remembered her conversation with her best friend well.

"You're turning into a prude," Stephanie had said over coffee.

"I'm not a prude. I just don't believe in *doing* every man in the county."

"I don't *do* everyone," Steph said, "I just have fun. And good, hot, sweaty sex is the most fun I can think of. I'm not married, I insist on condoms, and everyone knows the rules. What's really wrong with that?"

Elaine thought about it for a minute. When Steph said it, it sounded so reasonable. But it wasn't. Or was it?

"I can see the wheels turning," Steph continued. "You're unencumbered and over twenty-one. Come tomorrow night and just mingle. Do what you want, and no more. Loosen up. You can always leave."

"I don't think so."

"Elaine, look." Steph leaned forward. "I don't want you to violate any of your principles. You certainly don't have to come if you don't want to, and you know you'll still be my closest friend. But I want to share some of the fun with you. I've known you since grammar school and I know you'll have a blast if you just relax. So do what you want, and, if I don't see you tomorrow night, I'll call you next week."

So here she was at a party with several dozen good-looking people, all standing around, talking about politics and movies. Except for the fact that the clothes they wore were more flamboyant than the clothes she'd seen at other parties she'd been to, it really felt normal. It didn't look like a party that she knew was going to deteriorate into an orgy at any minute.

"Well, hello," a masculine voice said from behind her. "You

haven't been here before. I know. I would have remembered someone as gorgeous as you."

What a line, Elaine thought. So corny. "Hello," she said, turning and staring. God, he was good-looking, with soft, curly golden hair and deep blue eyes. Too bad he had such an awful line.

There was a moment of silence; then the man burst out laughing. "I just replayed my mental tape of that line I handed you. Wasn't that terrible?"

Elaine gasped, then smiled. "Yeah, it really was."

"Okay, let's start again. Hi. My name's Justin." He winked. "Now what? Should I use the 'What's your sign?' line now?"

Elaine liked his honesty. As she looked at his tall, muscular form, she liked him even better. She gazed as his hand, which was holding a glass of red wine. Long fingers and short, well-groomed nails. She was a sucker for hands, and she wondered suddenly how they would feel on her breasts. "Actually, I'm a Sagittarius, and my name's Elaine."

RAPE FANTASIES

Many women dream of being overpowered. Men fantasize about having absolute power. In a woman's version, all control is removed by some attractive man who ravishes her and, though she hates to admit it, makes her enjoy it. For a man, he controls a gorgeous woman, subdues her, and makes her love it.

These fantasies have *nothing* to do with the abhorrent crime of rape and really shouldn't even be described by the word *rape*. Most people who have rape fantasies wouldn't dream of ever carrying them through, of forcing anyone to do anything. But the fantasies exist in many of our minds, so let's indulge our deepest and sexiest dreams.

233

Many people have fantasies in which they are totally different from their real selves: the chief executive who dreams of being dominated by a powerful woman; the shy secretary whose nights are colored by fantasies of making a man do her bidding; the quiet couple who both play with the idea of controlling another couple's lovemaking.

If you've ever wanted to play with such a fantasy, here are the beginnings of two stories for you to embellish, alone or with your lover. One is written from a man's point of view and one from a woman's. Remember that these activities are nonconsensual, but they are, after all, only fantasies. If this idea doesn't appeal, turn to the next Saturday night.

HE RAVISHES

He saw that the woman was sleeping. It was a hot night, so she had obviously left the windows open, hoping for a slight breeze. As the night progressed, the wind had picked up and now the curtains flapped, the noise covering any sounds the stealthy intruder might make. He had climbed through the window and his feet had landed softly on the thick carpet. Now he looked from the sleeping woman around the moonlit room, searching for the elaborate wooden box in which he knew she kept an assortment of gaudy but expensive jewelry. He slowly removed a small penlight from his pocket and flashed its narrow beam around the dresser. Yes, he thought, there it is. Then he heard a sound from the bed. Damn, he thought, she wasn't supposed to wake up.

As the woman moved to sit up, the burglar strode to the bed and put his hand over her mouth, pressing her against the mattress. "Don't yell and I won't hurt you." He looked down at her wide eyes and saw her nod. "There's no one to hear you anyway. I made sure of that." As she nodded again, he ran his eyes over her gorgeous body. She was wearing only a sheer gown and, in the moonlight, it left little to the imagination.

Slowly, he raised his hand from her mouth, and as soon as she was free, she grabbed the sheet and pulled it up until it covered her from neck to toes. "J-j-just take the jewels and get out of here," she stammered.

He felt his body react to her fear and her near nakedness. He'd never before assaulted one of his robbery victims and he began to think through the possible consequences. As he did, he stared at the woman's eyes, watched her hands shake. His body urgently insisted on conquest. Yes, he thought, I might just do it.

SHE'S HELPLESS

"I hate to tell you this," Mr. Forsythe said. He was seated across the desk from her, his denim-clad legs crossed, his hands resting quietly in his lap. "I know all about your brother's embezzlement."

Diane was flabbergasted. The minor transgression had happened several years earlier and the money had been replaced without anyone but her knowing. Or at least she had always thought that no one else knew. "My brother never—"

"Don't insult us both with denials," he said. "We both know it's true. But only the two of us need to know."

"Listen, Mr. Forsythe," she said, "this is all silly, and I'd like you to leave my office right now."

"First of all, it's Thad, and second, I'll be leaving in just a few minutes. After you've heard my terms."

"Terms? For what?"

"You are going to have to buy my silence. I won't tell your

235

precious family anything about the ten thousand dollars. No one ever has to know. And it won't cost you much at all."

Diane glared at the man. He was so smug. So smooth. She wouldn't pay him a thing. Not a red cent. "I won't pay you anything."

"Oh, it's not money I want. It's you."

She stood up, furious. "What?"

"All you have to do for me to keep your little secret is show up at my house tonight. I want you. I have for a long time now, but until today, I didn't have the means to make you mine."

"Ridiculous. I'll do no such thing."

"Yes, I think you will. You know what? I'll make you enjoy it, too. You'll come to my house, we'll have dinner and a few drinks, and then you'll do whatever I want. We'll play, and tease, and make love until dawn. You'll scream your pleasure many times through-out the night. I guarantee it."

"Not a chance."

"Think about your brother. How do you think that stuffy firm he works for will react to the news that he's an embezzler?"

He paused, and Diane pictured her brother and the scandal the revelations would create. He'd be devastated. "You wouldn't."

The man raised a deep brown eyebrow over his almost-black eyes. "I would. But is it such a high price for you to pay for my silence?"

Diane swallowed hard. How far would this thing go? Would he really take her against her wishes? She looked at the hard planes of his face. Yes, he would. She sighed. Did she have a choice? She dropped back into her chair, her hands trembling.

"I'll take that for a yes. Wonderful. Here's my card." Thad handed Diane a small embossed business card. "Be at my house at seven tonight, and wear something formal. I will thoroughly enjoy peeling you out of it."

Diane looked at the card as Thad rose. She had no choice really. None. She stared at the card, already planning what to wear.

Saturday Night #48

Shave Where???

*T*onight, let's do something really daring. Have you ever wanted to go further and shave your entire genital area? Maybe you'd like to leave only a heart-shaped area of pubic hair as a few porn stars do. Or are you a man who wants to shave your genitals? It's not an uncommon desire. So for this Saturday night, shave part or all of your genital area.

Why? There are lots of reasons. It makes oral sex more pleasant for some and the sensations are exaggerated. Even the crotch of your jeans presses in different ways.

Many men are very turned on by the sight of a trimmed or shaved genital area, and some men shave their groin hair. It can also be surprisingly erotic to see your partner for the first time looking new and ready to love. A man or woman with naked genitals looks intentionally provocative, and that's exactly what you want.

237

Shaving each other can be a very sexy sharing of intimate touches and a demonstration of the trust you have in your partner and that your lover has in you. In addition, the shaver really gets to explore all the geography in a way he or she might not have before.

Why would someone want to shave? There are several reasons. First, it looks different, inviting, sexy. It looks like you are aware of your genitals and not afraid of them. You want to show off your desire for a good hot roll in the hay. For many, it makes asking a partner for oral sex easier, because one distraction is eliminated and many different sensations are possible.

Why not? Before you consider shaving, consider these warnings. First, when the hair grows back in, it itches like the very devil, as any woman who's ever been shaved before childbirth can tell you. Second, your groin is supersensitive and any infection, irritation, or inflammation will make your life a living hell for a few days. Wearing anything over that area will be extremely uncomfortable, and that includes jeans, panties, or panty hose. And sweat and natural wetness add to the problem. If you're reluctant about actually shaving, you can easily trim your pubic hair quite short with a pair of scissors, being very careful where you cut.

One more warning. There's a chance that you'll either nick or scratch yourself, so take care to avoid contact with another person's bodily fluids to eliminate the risk of disease transmission. Of course, if you're in doubt about your partner's sexual history, maybe you shouldn't shave at all.

Many women, myself included, now shave what's come to be known as their bikini line, the hair that grows on the inside of their thighs, outside the area normally covered by a bikini. I use an electric razor on those limited areas and haven't had any trouble. I will say that on the rare occasions that I decide to shave with a blade in the shower, I inevitably end up with an itchy and quite bothersome razor rash.

Therefore, if you decide to shave, there are several pieces of advice I can offer before you begin, gathered from various sources, including the visitors to my Web site who gladly offered their suggestions.

Here's the best way to go about it.

1. Before you begin, take a long, warm bath and relax. This will soften the hair and get the skin as clean as possible. Then wash the area thoroughly with an antibacterial soap.
2. Since shorter hair is easier for the razor to cope with, if you have long pubic hair, trim. Electric clippers or a pair of small, very sharp scissors work best.
3. Rinse the area with cool water, removing any clippings and cooling the skin.
4. Apply shaving cream a few minutes before shaving to soften the hair further. Consider using a shaving cream with additional conditioners or aloe. Warning: As with any product you're going to use near your most sensitive areas, test a bit of shaving cream on your wrist first to be sure there's no chance you'll react adversely. If you get any kind of redness or itching, don't use it.
5. When you're ready to begin shaving, get a sharp blade or a new disposable razor. You might try using two new blades if you are shaving a large area, and use a new razor every time you shave. The sharpest blade lessens any chance of scrapes and scratches and minimizes the number of passes you need to make over an area.

When shaving, stroke the razor no more than twice over the area in order to reduce skin irritation. Stroke first *with the grain* to remove most of the hair; then stroke *against the grain.* If you don't feel smooth enough, let it be and shave the area again in a few days. More scraping vastly increases the chance of irritation.

6. Be sure to wash afterward with soap and water to reduce the risk of infection and redness. Ideally, give the area a second cleansing using cotton balls and rubbing alcohol or aftershave lotion. It might sting a bit, but it's worth it to prevent discomfort later.

7. Be sure to shower or bathe daily, carefully washing the genitals to prevent infection. You might want to go so far as to keep a dispenser of antibacterial soap in the shower for just that purpose.

8. As to how often to shave, I've gotten a lot of conflicting advice. Some say wait as long as you can before shaving again; others maintain that it's easiest if you shave every day as part of your general routine. I guess it's a matter of how your body reacts and how you want to look.

There are other methods of hair removal that deserve negative mention here. Depilatories like Nair are designed to use on legs and arms. The packages specifically state that they are not for use on vaginal or perianal areas. Please take that warning seriously and don't use strong chemicals on delicate tissues.

In both waxing and a special technique known as sugaring, substances are applied, allowed to dry and/or harden, then pulled off. As with depilatories, these are also meant to be used on strong skin, like arms and legs, not on sensitive areas.

For Fun

♥♡If your lover wants to shave, how about helping or even offering to do it yourself? Help your lover feel sexy and desirable with music and scented candles. Make it an erotic activity by touching and licking others areas of his or her body while you

work. Take your time and smooth the shaving soap all over, even accidentally touching soapy hands to the perianal area. Admire the areas you're uncovering, using four-letter words if they are a turn-on. You might even want to shower together afterward, washing those newly exposed areas. Don't forget to use some aftershave or witch hazel when you finish.

A note: If you make love right after shaving, I would advise a shower or at least a thorough bathing of the area to clean away any lingering fluids. Those can lead to unnecessary discomfort.

Shaving can become a prelude to sex that will look and feel new, different, and exotic.

Saturday Night #49

Two's Company, Three's a Delicious Fantasy

As you already know, I have a very active Web site at http://www.joanelloyd.com, and I get dozens of questions each week on sexual topics. Many of them deal with threesomes. Usually the letter will say something like this: "My husband [wife] has always wanted to include our best friend in our lovemaking. I'd love to give it a try, but I'm not sure of the consequences. What's your opinion?"

Let me share my feelings, and then I'll tell you how to make a threesome into a delicious evening of lovemaking.

As for including another person in your relationship, I'm dead set against it. I have, of course, gotten letters from folks who've made it work. People live through auto accidents, too, but I wouldn't recommend it. Letting another person into your bedroom opens both of you up to jealousies, odious comparisons, and all manner of emotional problems.

Is he better than I am?

Does she have bigger breasts?

Now that she's made love with the other woman, will I ever be good enough for her?

He invited me to make love with the other man, but now will he be jealous?

Do I like him better?

Is she gay?

Is he gay?

And there are many, many more such questions. In spite of all this, the idea of a threesome is at the center of so many fantasies. Being pleasured by two men or two women at one time and/or watching your partner make love with another man or woman plays through your mind like an erotic movie. Threesomes are at the heart of many XXX-rated films for just this reason.

Okay, with my warnings in mind, how can you include a third in your bedroom? Through the power of the well-told story.

First, be sure that your partner is interested in this sort of fantasy. You don't want your lover to think that you're inventing another person because you're not satisfied with the one you've got. Nonsense. This is a game, played by only two people. Once you're sure that both of you want to play, here's how it might begin.

For Both of You

♥♡ Snuggle in bed together tonight and turn out all the lights. Hold hands and maybe share a glass of wine in the dark.

Together, create a fictional person to invite in. Don't use anyone you know, since you'll never be able to look that person in the eye again. Don't use a movie star, since this might lead to jealousy when you next go to the movies. Just build the person together.

Take care to avoid comparisons, even with an imaginary person. Does she have bigger breasts than I have? she might be thinking. Is he sexier? Here's a cute way to avoid even that type of comparison. How about a fantasy involving a clone of your partner. Maybe a mad scientist has created the clone and he or she's entering the bedroom right now. Hmm. Delicious thought? Or just tell the story and forget any description, so that each person can imagine a dream individual.

Let's assume that you two want to create another man and invite him into the bedroom. It might go like this:

"I'd love to have another man join us for a night of terrific fantasy sex. Maybe we'll invite him to play with us."

"Sure. What's his name?"

"Let's call him Greg." (Again, stay away from the name of anyone you know, just to be on the safe side.)

"Okay. He's standing in the bedroom door, silhouetted against the bright light in the hall. He sees us in bed together and he's just watching."

"Hello, Greg."

The fantasy's begun. Where does it go from here? Anywhere you want it to. You each can play a part. You can pretend to be any of the characters in the story.

Want to have an orgy with another couple? Do it the same way.

Want to go to a sex club, get nude, and make love with several people at once? There's a way to accomplish that, too. It's your joint fantasy.

For Fun

♥♡ To add to the experience, change sides of the bed before starting. It's amazing how patterns take over our lovemaking. Break one of them, and it's easier to become someone else, if only for a short while.

Saturday Night # 50

Back-Door Play

W e've graduated to more adventurous activities, and I know this night won't be for everyone. Tonight, we're going to explore a topic regarded as taboo by many: anal sex. If this isn't for you, flip back and select another night. For many, this is an exciting type of bedroom play.

Many men and women enjoy anal sex, and I will admit that both Ed and I play from time to time. But there are many warnings and bits of advice you will need before you begin. If you're experienced, you might find something new here, too.

Why is anal sex so exciting? I think there are several reasons. There are lots of nerve endings around the anus that are stimulated during anal play, and the anus is close neighbor to all the nerve endings in the genitals. Also, since the opening of the anus is so tight, if a man inserts his penis into a woman's anus, it really squeezes the penis and holds it in a tight sheath. Anal sex is, however, one of the most basic taboos, one that we can ignore if we choose.

Why is it such a taboo? In some religions, any form of intercourse that doesn't lead to procreation is prohibited, thus making this a forbidden activity. For whatever reason, it's one of the biggest no-nos there is. And that's really too bad because it's an activity that is enjoyable for so many.

Anal intercourse, in which a man inserts his penis into the rectum, is the least common form of anal sex. For many men and women, a touch or light massage during sex play is enough to stimulate additional pleasure centers. For others, inserting a slim dildo or vibrator or even a finger can make sparks fly.

How to Begin

You might begin the same way you began to understand your penis or vagina, by touching yourself to see what's pleasurable. In the shower or tub, touch your anus. You'll probably find that, although it's scary, it's an exciting experience. Explore and see what you like.

Once you've discovered that anal stimulation is exciting for you, it's time to introduce the idea to your partner. Tread gently, but do mention it. Slip it into a story or show your partner an anal dildo in a catalog. You might even let your fingers stray toward that sensitive area next time you're playing, in order to gauge your lover's reaction. Or direct your partner's fingers to yours. You might be very surprised.

A word of warning. As with any activity, don't play if you're even slightly repelled by the idea. Don't do it just to please your partner. You have the responsibility to say no. However, if that "no" response is a knee-jerk reaction—"I don't want to even

think about this; it's just too kinky"—take a moment, and a deep breath; then respond.

Now what? Okay, you've ascertained that you both are interested, so how do you integrate this activity into your lovemaking? Begin with simple anal stimulation during sex play. See whether it's as wonderful as you thought it would be. Let your lover gently rub your anal opening with a lubricated finger. Don't penetrate just yet; take a while to get used to the idea first. Share the knowledge that there will be no penetration with your partner if he or she is new to anal games. If you charge ahead now, you're more likely to have problems. If touching was exciting, it's time for another step forward.

ANAL PENETRATION

The decision as to what to use to penetrate the anus is up to you. Use a finger or try a slender dildo or vibrator specifically designed for anal play, one with a large flange around the base so it won't get lost. The anal passage is not closed at the interior end like the vagina, so objects can be inserted so far that they require a trip to the emergency room to be removed. Not the way you want to end your lovemaking evening! Anal dildos and vibrators can be purchased through any sex-toy catalog or Web site.

Whichever you choose, get warmed up first with lots of kissing, petting, and stroking to get both of you very excited. The idea of anal play gets easier as you both get hotter.

Use lots of lubricant. And I do mean *lots*. While the vagina and penis both produce lubricating fluid, the anus does not. This means that it won't get any slipperier than it is right now, even with rubbing. So use plenty of lube, and add more as needed. Take care not to insert a finger that's been in contact with the anal area back into a jar or bottle of lubricant or even let it come in contact with the rim of the tube. There are lots of very dangerous bacteria in the anus and you don't want to spread them around—ever. In addition to lubricating whatever is to be inserted, spread lots of slippery stuff around the anal opening, as well. Most lubricants are cold and feel delicious.

If you want to use a finger to penetrate your partner, put on a latex glove and then add lots of lubricant. Be sure your nails are trimmed, and be gentle. You can then remove the glove when you are ready to move to another activity.

Here's another idea. Cover the dildo or finger with a well-lubricated condom and then play. This allows you to remove the condom and play vaginally later on. And, as I've said before and can't stress enough, never, under any circumstances, let anything that's been in contact with the anal area come in contact with vaginal tissues.

Relax. Take your time.

When you're both ready, insert the dildo or finger just a bit; then wait. It will be a bit painful at first, but once the anal muscles relax and get used to the object, it should become pleasurable. Just remember, this isn't an endurance contest. If it doesn't become enjoyable in short order, stop and, if you like, try again another time.

Once the dildo or finger is inserted and the muscles relax, withdraw and insert, simulating intercourse. For a woman, this is pleasure enough to excite and to satisfy. For a man, you might try rubbing his prostate, a dome-shaped gland found about two inches from the opening, on the belly side of the passage. Many find that anal play can lead to orgasm almost as quickly as vaginal play, and they find those orgasms can be even stronger.

If you've progressed to trying to insert your penis into her anus, use two condoms. Anal intercourse is a high-risk sexual

activity and the danger of disease transmission can't be over-stated. I would never have intercourse with anyone I suspected of carrying any disease, but I would be doubly careful with anal play.

Remember to add lots of lubricant, a specific product designed for this purpose. I know many of you are skipping around in this book, so, at the risk of repeating myself, I say again, no petroleum products near condoms. They create tiny holes and permit passage of all things the condoms are designed to keep out.

Allow the one who's being penetrated to control the play. Remember that he or she is the one enjoying a new sensation and will know how deep, how fast, and how hard. This is supposed to be pleasurable for both of you, so slow down and let the receiver lead. And please, receiver, do just that. Help your partner to make this as enjoyable as it can be for you both.

Don't forget other forms of stimulation while you play. Touch her breasts and clitoris; touch his penis and testicles to increase the heat.

What positions work best for anal intercourse?

♡ A good way to start is for her to straddle him, thus being in complete control of the penetration. She can either face him or turn toward his feet; then either of you can hold and guide his penis toward the opening. With her on her knees, she can slowly lower her body onto his erect penis.

♡ Another good position is for her to lie on her side and curl her knees up. Then he can lie behind, spoon-style.

♡ Doggie-style positions the woman on all fours, with the man behind. A variation of this is for her to pull her knees up beneath her belly.

♡ She can lie on her back with her knees pulled as close to her chest as possible.

♡ The two can stand, with her bent over and him behind.

249

There is an additional problem with anal intercourse. The man must maintain a very hard erection in order to penetrate and stay inside an anus. For many men, this is difficult, especially when new to this kind of play. Even if he wants to try it, those taboos go very deep. So if it doesn't happen the first time, there's a good chance it will improve in later attempts.

If you want to start by reading stories about couples who enjoy anal sex, try http://www.analstories.com/zagnut.html. For pictures and advice, try http://www.ab-cybersex.com/anal experience/default.html. And if you want to look at pictures of people enjoying anal sex, use any search engine and search on the topic "Anal Sex." You'll find hundreds of sites, so click around until you find one with photos that make your heart beat faster.

For Fun

❤♡ Here's a position that you will enjoy. Let her rest only the top half of her body on the bed, with her knees on a pillow on the floor next to the bed. Then play.

For Fun

❤♡ As you get more used to anal play, graduate to larger dildos if that pleases. You can also use a dildo in one passage while he inserts his penis into the other.

Not everyone gets enjoyment from anal play, and if you don't, that's fine. Just don't let your knee-jerk reactions get in the way of some unusual fun. It's just that simple.

Saturday Night #51

I Can't Answer the Phone Right Now; I'm All Tied Up

Bondage. Tying each other up. It's a game that many people, Ed and I included, enjoy tremendously. And it's the most basic of power games, which we'll discuss in more depth in the final Saturday night.

When I began to experiment with unusual sex, bondage was the first thing I tried. It was difficult for me to admit that I had always wanted to surrender control during sex, but the communication I had developed with my partner made this admission possible. Why was it so hard to do? I had thought that bondage was a kinky activity and just too far out for a forty-some-year-old woman to try. Lucky for me, my partner quickly informed me otherwise. And I will be forever glad I did try it.

Why? Let me try to explain.

For the one who's tied, there's complete freedom from responsibility. "If I'm tied up, I don't have to worry about what I'm supposed to do, because I have no choices to make. I merely have to lie here and accept whatever my partner wants to do, or use the safe word to stop things."

For the one who's doing the tying, it's complete freedom, since you have your partner's word of honor that he or she will use the safe word to stop things if anything gets uncomfortable. "I can do anything I like since I know my partner will say 'red' if things get bad."

For most power games, and bondage specifically, you need to agree to one basic thing before you start: a safe word. A safe word is a word you two decide upon that, when said, means that everything stops. Immediately and without question. The word should be something that wouldn't ordinarily be used in conversation. Say "Tabasco" or "dandelion," or the simple, commonly used "red."

If you're the one being tied up, you must *promise* to use it if things get the least bit uncomfortable. If you're nervous, uncomfortable, in pain, or if your foot's merely asleep, use it. It's your job!

If you can't trust your partner to use the safe word at even the slightest hint of displeasure, don't play.

If you're the one doing the tying, you must promise to stop whatever's going on immediately when that safe word is used. Without question or hesitation!

If you can't trust your partner to stop the moment the safe word is used, don't play.

If you can agree to these simple rules, give it a try.

Have you ever wondered whether your partner might like to be tied up? The simplest way to find out is to ask. Mention it in a story and gauge your lover's reaction. If you don't want to ask, however, here's a way you might get a clue. During lovemaking, hold your partner's wrists and see how he or she reacts. If you want to go further, stretch your lover's arms over his or her head or straight out at the shoulders and hold them taut. Does it make your lover hot? If so, that might mean that he or she would enjoy being restrained. Ask you lover. Discuss it fully. It's really difficult to begin such a conversation, but without full understanding and agreement, you cannot go any further.

Do you tremble with excitement at the idea of being bound? Does you heart pound? Do your palms get sweaty? Take the risk and tell your partner. Slip the idea into a fantasy tale or buy a small bondage toy, a piece of rope, or a short length of chain and a lock. Bring it up no matter now difficult! You might be the brave one who finally uncovers the fact that you and your lover have the same ideas.

Now that you've decided to play, start small. Here are several ways to make bondage into a game and make the game less threatening.

♡ Tie your lover up with a piece of thread. Obviously, he or she can break the "bonds" anytime, but suggest that your partner play along. "It's a piece of magic thread," you can say, "stronger than any steel cable. And you can't break it no matter how hard you pull." Now you've created a bondage situation that's only as real as you want to make it.

♡ Have your partner put his or her hands on the headboard of the bed and play "don't let go." This can become a game to see whether you can get your lover so excited he or she will let go of the bed.

♡ Have your lover pretend that his or her hands are held down by thousand-pound weights. "You can't move that weight, so you're at my mercy."

In all of these games, your partner is really free to end things at any time. But it's much more fun to let things go on.

If you've tried nonbondage games and want to go for the real thing, here are a few caveats. Be sure not to tie your partner in any way that cannot be loosened quickly in an emergency. Nothing will ruin the mood like the sound of a child coughing when you can't get loose to check. Check often to be sure the bonds aren't too tight. Sometimes in the heat of passion, we forget to notice that hands or feet have become numb. Be aware.

253

Don't play martyr. If something's painful, use the safe word and ask your partner to redo or untie. Bondage games are supposed to bring you both sexual pleasure. You can't enjoy yourself if you're uncomfortable, and when your partner finds out that's how you felt, he or she will feel sorry. There are ways to be bound up without being in pain.

Don't run out and buy expensive equipment. Unless you're wealthy or want to get something outrageous for a gift, there are many inexpensive ways to play. For example:

♡ Scarves and old nylon stockings work well for bindings. Don't use anything narrow, however, like twine or cord, since that can cut off circulation and do damage.

♡ Get a length of very soft rope from the local hardware store. If you're embarrassed, claim that you're going to use it for a clothesline. Cut the rope into five- or ten-foot lengths so that you can reach whatever you want to tie together.

♡ You can find collars of all sizes in the pet department of any store. Four of these, two for wrists and two for ankles, work wonderfully, and the smell of leather can add to the other sensations.

♡ Chains are incredibly sexy. They are the ultimate unbreakable bonds, are delightfully cold, and the sound they make when dropped into the palm is really erotic. The pet department will have inexpensive metal choke collars for dogs and cats of all sizes, and these are nothing but heavy chains. Get a few and, if you need to, pretend you have a dog. Those clips that connect leashes to collars can also hook the rings on collars together.

♡ Padlocks have a deep significance. There's a finality to being locked into a chain or collar. Small padlocks can be purchased at hardware or luggage stores. Be sure to keep the key handy in case of emergency.

♡ I find that something tight around my waist adds to the illusion of being completely bound. A belt or length of Ace bandage works fine. Just be sure not to make anything too tight.

Don't get hung up on one way of tying your partner up. Having your lover lie spread-eagle on the bed is the most common, but tying your partner's elbows to his or her wrists, or wrists to ankles, works well, too. There are Web sites with bondage pictures for you to use as models if you run out of ideas.

A word of advice: It's almost impossible to lie on your back comfortably while your wrists are tied behind you, so if want your partner lying down, tie his or her wrists to the headboard of the bed or the leg of a sofa.

There are myriad Web sites devoted to bondage activities. If you're interested, try:

- http://us.1porn.com/bondmag: Bondage magazines.
- http:www.snapit.com/BDSM-online-magazine.html: A newspaper, magazines, videos, and fetish equipment.

Or you can search any of the engines by typing in "bondage" or "BDSM" (for bondage and discipline, sadomasochism). There are additional resources at the end of the next Saturday night.

For Fun

❤♡Tie your partner's wrists together loosely, then go out for a drive in the car. If you two are careful, no one will see anything. Going through the drive-through at McDonald's, however, becomes an erotic experience.

Most important, the first and last rule is that bondage is never used to force anyone to do anything. This is mutual pleasure and nothing else. Period.

Saturday Night #52

The Power of Power

Last Saturday night, we played with the most basic power game, bondage. Tonight, we're going to go a bit further. If you haven't already read the section for last Saturday night, please read it now and agree on a safe word with your partner. Once you do, you can play any type of power game you want.

What exactly are power games? These are sex games that create an unbalanced relationship. One person controls the action and one is somewhat, if not completely, passive. Why play? I've talked about giving up control, but let me take a moment to explain why being in control can also be so liberating. Although when playing power games, I usually like to be the one controlled, I do, on occasion, take control of lovemaking with Ed. I "order" him to lie still and let me do all the work. Then, in addition to doing what I know he likes, sometimes I try something different, something we've never done before.

I've spanked him, tried anal sex, and initiated several other new diversions. I know that he will use the safe word if I go too far, so I can do whatever tickles my fancy. I can leave my usual self behind and be different, bold, and daring.

I can also "order" him to do something to me. If I'm in the mood for a long session of oral sex, I can say, "I want you to lick me until I allow you to stop." If I want a quickie, I can tell him, "Fuck me now!" Being in control is a license to be selfish. And sometimes my being selfish is wonderful for us both.

There's yet another benefit. When I'm in control, Ed listens very carefully to what I ask for, adding it to his mental list of the things I enjoy. Need I say more?

Realize, too, that control games aren't gender-specific. Either partner can assume control, become the dominant, or "top," and either partner can give up control and become the submissive, or "bottom."

How to Explore

There are hundreds of variations on control games. Here are a few you might like to begin with:

♡ Feed your partner a love potion that will make him or her your love slave. As long as your partner plays along, you're in control.

♡ Say to your partner, with an appropriate leer, "I'm sorry I was bad today. Maybe you can figure a way that I can make it up to you."

♡ Go through an erotic video and select a scene that you and your partner *must* reenact.

♡ One of you can light a candle and say, "This is a magic candle.

257

As long as it's lit, you are mine to do whatever I like." With a grin and an imaginary twirled mustache, the fun begins.

♡ Find an erotic story to act out. One great Web site for mind-control stories is http://www.mcstories.com. Please note that all these stories are fantasies about nonconsensual sex, so read with that in mind. They will, however, give you lots of ideas for fantasies involving one partner having absolute power over the other.

If you're new to playing games, keep the rest of the love-making simple for a few sessions. Save the anal sex, hot wax, or a slap on the bottom for another time. The power game itself is different enough, and you don't want to make this a scary experience. The kind of trust that's needed to indulge fully in games of control must be built over time. If you take baby steps, the process is much more likely to lead into fascinating realms of unusual and creative sex.

In addition to power games, there are other bedroom activities we haven't yet explored. There are so many ways that people make love or use objects that they enjoy playing with, I won't try to mention them all. You can let your fingers do the walking over the Internet and learn about many of them. Here are just a few.

PAIN AS PLEASURE

There are lots of people who enjoy pain as sexual stimulation or gratification. Whips and paddles are commonly sold toys for bedroom games. A simple slap on the buttocks during sex play can tell you whether this is an area you might want to explore.

FETISHES

Let's take a moment to discuss a word that carries so many layers of meaning that it's almost impossible to use without getting judgmental. The word *fetish* is commonly used for any object with a sexual attachment—from high-heeled shoes to feathers—that stimulates sex in a way that's unusual or out of the norm, whatever that is. Here's my take on it. Anything that's done or used by consenting adults is none of anyone else's business. Some toys are just a shade different; many are really unusual. But that's the business of those involved. Period.

Let's be clear about who is a *consenting adult.* A consenting adult is someone who understands the difference between yes and no, and who knows that either is an acceptable choice at any time. A consenting adult understands that sex is not to be performed with anyone who doesn't understand and agree to this. A consenting adult can agree to a safe word and will use it and abide by it in all circumstances, no matter how difficult. Since drugs and alcohol affect the ability and/or desire to consent, have all discussions and make all agreements completely sober and drug-free.

If you and your partner are both consenting adults, whatever you want to try is fine. There are sexual activities out there that would amaze you and many that would probably make you uncomfortable. So see what feels good, and reject what doesn't.

If you're interested in pursuing your interest in power games or other unusual bed sports, go the the Internet and click over to:

- http://www.bdsmcafe.com
- http://www.cuffs.com: DS Kiosk: A resource center for dominants and submissives.

- http://www.dragscape.com: Michelle's Midday Break—a great transgender resource.
- http://www.fetish.com
- http://www.fetishindex.com: Links to over 2000 sites of every kind.
- http://gloria-brame.com: Castle in the Sky—an eclectic literary site for freethinkers.
- http://www.leatherquest.com
- http://www.portlandplace.com/portland/splash.htm
- http://www.smartweb.net/~raven: Wonderful essays and such on alternative sex play (the site comes up a bit strangely, but it's worth the annoyance).
- http://www.thespankingpage.com: Lots of links to like-minded sites
- http://www.ultspank.com

You can, of course, use any of the search engines by keying in "Spanking," "Fetish," "Water Sports," or whatever else intrigues you. I searched on Yahoo using "BDSM" and I found links to literally hundreds of sites devoted to all forms of off-center sex play. By the way, many of these sites aren't in English, so surf accordingly.

Remember, you don't have to indulge in any of these activities, but it might be exciting to explore.

Conclusion

e've been together for fifty-two Saturday nights. One year of sexual communication and experimentation. One year of learning what pleases and what doesn't. One year of talking and laughing and making mistakes. One year of discovering new activities to spice up your bedroom, your living room, and kitchen. One year to reinforce the truth that it's the journey that's the joy, not just the destination.

Now you're on your own. Does that mean that you've no more use for this book? Not really. Maybe there were ideas that didn't appeal when you read them the first time that deserve a second or a third look. Maybe there were special sections that lead to extraordinary evenings.

Revisit any and all Saturday nights here—often. Don't let the things you've discovered slip into the background under the noise of everyday living.

Here's a fun way to use this book. Use a deck of cards as indicators of the fifty-two Saturday nights. Clubs stand for the first quarter of the year, diamonds the second, hearts the third, and spades the fourth. So a four of diamonds is the fourth night of the second quarter, "Afterglow," Saturday Night #17; the ace of spades the first night of the fourth quarter, "Betcha," Saturday Night #40; and so on. Just pick a card, turn to that page, and voilà. Make the game a regular part of your lovemaking and play perhaps once a month. If there are nights you didn't want to revisit, remove the appropriate card. If there were special ones you'd like to do again and again, mark that card for easier selection. Cheating? Sure. But who cares?

If you've got ideas that I didn't mention, comments, or questions of any kind, please write to me. I'll get back to you as quickly as I can. In addition, your comments might help another couple enhance their lovemaking. I'm always adding new material to my Web site, much of it from readers and visitors like you. I'd love to add your thoughts—anonymously, of course.

You can reach me at:

Joan Elizabeth Lloyd
Post Office Box 221
Yorktown Heights, NY 10598

Or: joan@joanelloyd.com

And please visit my Web site at http://www.joanelloyd.com and enjoy the myriad comments and suggestions. In addition, I post a new erotic story each month, and I add frequent essays on sexual topics, too.

My final wish for you is that your next fifty-two Saturday nights will prove as adventurous and wonderful as the last ones have been.

Appendix

There are myriad sites on the Internet devoted to sexuality in all forms, and I've listed many throughout this book. Below, I've collected all the addresses and Web sites mentioned for your quick reference. Obviously, my list wasn't exhaustive, and so these are just examples of what's out there. Be prepared for the occasional error message, indicating that the site you're trying to access doesn't exist anymore. If you get such a message, and you've typed the address correctly, move on to another location.

Remember that sites seldom limit their activities to one, so for the majority of these addresses, you'll find more than one type of material. Be flexible. Wander from page to page, and from link to link. Have a blast.

Appendix

CHILD PROTECTION SOFTWARE
- http://www.cyberpatrol.com
- http://www.cybersitter.com
- http://www.netnanny.com
- http://www.surfwatch.com

SEARCH ENGINES
- http://www.altavista.digital.com
- http://www.excite.com
- http://www.hotbot.com
- http://www.infoseek.com
- http://www.lycos.com
- http://www.webcrawler.com
- http://www.yahoo.com

SITES WITH LINKS TO OTHER ADULT SITES
- http://aosotd.com
- http://www.adult10000.com
- http://www.persiankitty.com
- http://www.sextop1000.com/index.html
- http://www.thexxxreview.com

AROMATHERAPY INFORMATION
- http://www.aromaweb.com
- http://www.fragrant.demon.co.uk
- http://www.zuzuspetals.net

AROMATHERAPY OIL PURCHASES
- http://www.crystalmountain.com
- http://www.evb-aromatherapy.com
- http://moonrise.botanical.com/aroma/aroma.html

- http://www.poyanaturals.com

SITES WITH INFORMATION OF INTEREST TO ADULT WEB SURFERS

- http://www.bodyandbath.mb.ca: Bath products.
- http://www.condomania.com: Condoms.
- http://www.csense.com: Condom Sense.
- http://www.euromode.com/rp/index.htm
- http://www.freelove.com/sex
- http://www.masturbationpage.com: The Masturbation Home Page.
- http://www.mentertainment.com/video/101-202.htm: Batteries Not Included.
- http://www.nonpiercingjewelry.com
- http://playcouples.com: The Lifestyles Organization.
- http://www.razberry.com/raz/pink/top.htm: Pink Kink.
- http://www.safersex.org/: The Safer Sex Organization.
- http://www.santesson.com/aphrodis/aphrhome.htm: The Aphrodisiac Home Page.
- http://www.sexuality.org: The Society for Human Sexuality.
- http://www.virtualflowers.com

SITES THAT CAN SEND ADULT GREETING CARDS

- http://www.angelfire.com/tx/oscarwilly
- http://www.bobkat.net/previewb.html
- http://www.clpw.net/eroticcards
- http://www.eroticcity.net/postcards/cardcenter.html
- http://www.eroticadreams.com/cards/card/html
- http://www.eroticpostcards.com
- http://www.kinkycards.com
- http://www.naughtycards.com
- http://www.southerncharms-ent.com/sce/postcards/postcard.html
- http://www.strip-a-gram.com

NEWSGROUP INFORMATION

- http://www.dejanews.com

NEWSGROUPS OF ADULT INTEREST
- alt.sex
- alt.sex.stories.moderated
- alt.sex.bondage
- alt.stories.erotic
- rec.arts.erotica

EROTIC STORY SITES
- http://www.adultstorycorner.com
- http://www.annejet.pair.com
- http://www.cadvision.com/jove
- http://www.connectx.com/cyntil8ing
- http://www.mcstories.com
- http://www.nifty.org
- http://www.pair.com/~julie
- http://users.lanminds.com/~mohanraj/home.html
- http://www.xstories.com

LINGERIE CATALOGS AND SITES
- Frederick's of Hollywood, PO Box 229, Hollywood, CA 90078-0229; 1-800-323-9525; http://www.fredericks.com
- Victoria's Secret, PO Box 16589, Columbus, OH 43216-6589; 1-800-888-8200; http://www.victoriassecret.com

ADULT MALLS
- http://www.pricebusters.com
- http://www.sexmall.com
- http://www.tcmd.com/app/index.html

TOYS AND ADULT PRODUCTS
- http://www.1adultsextoystore.com
- http://www.a-romantic.com: A soft-core site that might be a good place to begin.

- Adam and Eve, PO Box 800, Carrboro, NC 27510; 1-800-274-0333; http://www.aeonline.com
- http://www.adultatrium.com
- Alisha's Luvtoys, VMU, 11757 W. Ken Caryl Avenue, Suite F 210, Littleton, CO 80127; 1-800-932-7014 (United States only); www.luvtoys.com
- http://www.bedroomsports.com: A good on-line-only store.
- http://www.castlesuperstore.com: Castle Superstore is an on-line company that also has ten store locations throughout the United States. Their site also has a huge link list, including many sex search engines and lots of erotica sites.
- http://www.eroticsextoys.com
- Eve's Garden, 119 West 57th Street, #420, New York, NY 10019; 1-800-848-3837; http://www.evesgarden.com
- Good Vibrations, 938 Howard Street, Suite 101, San Francisco, CA 94103; 1-800-289-8423 (Mon.–Sat. 7:A.M.–7:00 P.M.—PT); http://www.goodvibes.com
- Intimate Treasures, PO Box 77902, San Francisco, CA 94107; 1-415-863-5002; http://www.intimatetreasures.com
- http://www.thepleasurechest.com
- http://www.sextoyshoppers.com
- The Xandria Collection (catalogs cost $2–$5, depending on the content), PO Box 319005, San Francisco, CA 94131-9988; 1-800-242-2823; http://www.xandria.com

VIDEOS
- http://www.69redhot.com
- http://www.adultsexfilms.com
- http://www.dvdflix.com/dvd/adult_lobby.asp
- http://www.excaliburfilms.com
- Leisure Time Products, PO Box M827, Gary, IN 46401-9900; 1-800-874-8960

- http://www.royalle.com
- VCI, PO Box 5185, Willowick, OH 44095, 1-800-886-3410 (11:00 A.M.–9:00 P.M.—ET)
- http://www.stggroup.com

LINK SITES TO ADULT SPECIALTIES
- http://fetish1000.com
- http://www.gay1000.com
- http://www.lesbian1000.com
- http://www.palace.com/exchan: Bondage and fetish links.

SPECIALTY ITEMS
- Brazen Images, PO Box 731, Hartsdale NY 10530-0731; 1-914-949-2605; http://www.brazenimages.com
- DeMars Sexy Footwear, Cypress Footwear, and USA Shoes and Boots, 11542 Knott Street, Unit B-7, Garden Grove, CA 92841; 1-714-903-2502; http://www.usashoes.com
- Dream Dresser, PO Box 16158, Beverly Hills, CA 90209-2158; 1-213-848-3480; http://www.dreamdresser.com
- Fashion World International, 9777 Business Park Drive, Suite C, Sacramento, CA 95827; 1-916-631-8777; http://www.fantasyfashion.com
- Leather for Lovers, PO Box 78550, San Francisco, CA 94107-8550; 1-415-863-4822; http://www.voyages.com
- Romantic Fantasy, Donnelly Enterprises, 8320 Denise Drive, Seminole, FL 33777; 1-727-393-9646 (Mon.–Thurs. 7:00 A.M.–10:30 A.M.—ET); http://www.jampacked.com

AMATEURS ON THE WEB
- http://www.100top.com/amateur/index.html
- http://www.amateur1000.com

NUDE CELEBRITY PHOTOS

- http://www.nudecelebritystars.com
- http://www.theharem.com
- http://www.mufflist.com

EROTIC GAMES FOR PURCHASE OR DOWNLOAD

- http://www.erotic-games.com
- http://www.firstfantasies.com

STORIES, INFORMATION, AND PICTURES ABOUT ANAL SEX

- http://www.analstories.com/zagnut.html
- http://www.ab-cybersex.com/analexperience/default.html

INFORMATION, TOYS, AND PICTURES FOR THOSE INTERESTED IN ADVANCED ACTIVITIES

- http://www.bdsmcafe.com
- http://www.cuffs.com
- http://www.dragscape.com
- http://www.fetish.com
- http://www.fetishindex.com
- http://www.gloria-brame.com
- http://www.leatherquest.com
- http://www.portlandplace.com/portland/splash.htm
- http://www.smartweb.net/~raven
- http://www.snapit.com/BDSM-online-magazine.html
- http://www.thespankingpage.com
- http://us.sexjam.com/bondmag